# The Miracle
of Love

# The Miracle of Love

Mother Teresa of Calcutta,
Her Missionaries of Charity,
and her Co-Workers

Kathryn Spink

**HARPER & ROW, PUBLISHERS**

SAN FRANCISCO

Cambridge
Hagerstown
Philadelphia
New York

1817

London
Mexico City
São Paulo
Sydney

Originally published in Great Britain in 1981 under the title *For the Brotherhood of Man under the Fatherhood of God* by Colour Library International, Ltd.

THE MIRACLE OF LOVE. Copyright © 1981 by Colour Library International, Ltd. All rights reserved. Printed in Spain. No part of this book may be used or reproduced in any manner whatsoever without written permission except in the case of brief quotations embodied in critical articles and reviews. For information address Harper & Row, Publishers, Inc., 10 East 53rd Street, New York, NY 10022.

FIRST U.S. EDITION

LC: 81-47717

ISBN: 0-06-067497-0

81  82  83  84  85  10  9  8  7  6  5  4  3  2  1  D.L.B.24.095-81

To Ann Blaikie,
without whom this book and many other things
would not have been possible.

# ACKNOWLEDGMENTS

It would be impossible to thank individually all those who have contributed to the production of a book of this kind. I would, however, like to take this opportunity of saying a very special "thank you" to Mother Teresa for giving me permission to delve into her "archives." "Thank you" also to Mrs Ann Blaikie, who invited a stranger into her home for one day and found she had adopted a semi-resident for several months, and to all the many other Co-Workers who in an invaluable and sometimes indefinable way gave of their energy, their resources and their hospitality.

In particular, I would like to thank Mlle Jacqueline de Decker for giving me a very special view of the many faces of Antwerp, Miss Alice Grattan-Esmonde for providing the opportunity to listen to tapes of Mother Teresa into the early hours of a Dublin morning, and Mrs Margaret Mackenzie for her help in general and especially for the use of her artwork. To Sister Marie-Celine MC, Sister Jose-Ann MC, Mrs Bunty Watts, Mr Tom Sweeney, Mrs Pauline Bethel and Mrs Evelyn Armitstead – again my sincere thanks for their assistance and support.

Finally, I would like to reiterate more formally my gratitude to Aloka Das who undertook so successfully to seek out information and take photographs in Calcutta, to Frances Brown who had the unenviable task of typing the manuscript and to my long-suffering husband who bore with me throughout.

# CONTENTS

If sometimes our poor people have had to die of starvation, it is not because God didn't care for them, but because you and I didn't give, were not instruments of love in the hands of God, to give them that bread, to give them that clothing; because we did not recognize him, when once more Christ came in distressing disguise – in the hungry man, in the lonely man, in the homeless child, and seeking for shelter.

God has identified himself with the hungry, the sick, the naked, the homeless; hunger, not only for bread, but for love, for care, to be somebody to someone; nakedness, not of clothing only, but nakedness of that compassion that very few people give to the unknown; homelessness, not only just for a shelter made of stone, but that homelessness that comes from having no one to call your own.

To show great love for God and our neighbor we need not do great things. It is how much love we put in the doing that makes our offering something beautiful for God.

MOTHER TERESA OF CALCUTTA

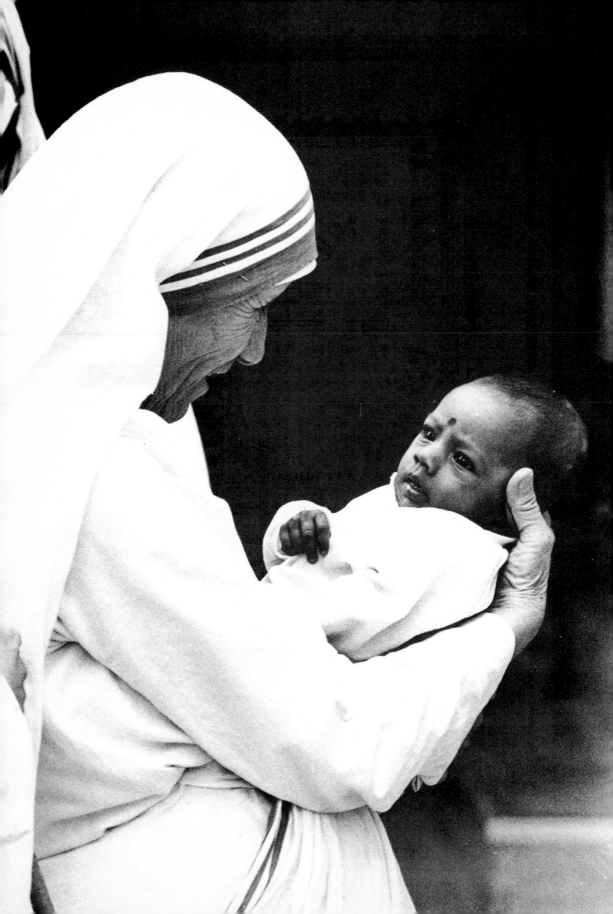

# God has saved us and called us with a holy calling, not in virtue of our works, but in virtue of his own purpose and the grace which he gave us in Christ Jesus ages ago.

(2 TIMOTHY 1:9)

Removed from the filth and squalor of one of Calcutta's three thousand "bustees", or slums, a gaunt-eyed woman lies dying in the gentle tranquility of Nirmal Hriday, Mother Teresa's home for dying destitutes – a small haven of cleanliness and peace in a city which has been described as "the slum of the world". Here, in the soft and somehow beautiful half-light which falls from small windows high up in the walls onto the rows of low beds, she watches as a small, slim figure dressed in a white sari bordered with blue, tends to her emaciated body – an almost fleshless frame consumed by disease and maggots. The stench which rises from those terrible wounds and sores is overpowering but the cleansing process continues. The face of the slight figure stooping over them shows no sign of repugnance, only an expression of love and joy, and when her patient, who is a Hindu, asks, in accordance with the rituals of her faith, that water from the sacred River Ganges be sprinkled on her lips, the request is readily granted. The woman from the "bustees", who has lived like an animal in the streets, dies with a dignity that

*"Any work of love brings a person face to face with God."*

11

transcends what might be considered natural human reactions. Her last words as she smiles up into a face lined by the suffering of thousands are not, as might be expected, a complaint or a cry for attention: "I'm hungry" or "I'm in such terrible pain", not even an expression of protest: "Why in a city which like so many others, has its wealth, its beauty and its culture, should I have had to scratch for a miserable existence in a disease-ridden slum, where there is no regular refuse collection and no filtered water supply?" Instead, with her dying breath she murmurs, "thank you". In the words of Mother Teresa she has died "like an angel".

To some who witness, perhaps for the first time, scenes such as this it is difficult to identify which are the true "angels" – the dying destitutes who apparently suffer so selflessly and unprotestingly or Mother Teresa and her helpers who move serenely and with such seemingly incongruous joy from one wound to the next. For others, who find it difficult to come to terms with the "angelic", to use such an expression is to move automatically into the realms of unreality, yet ironically, to lose sight of the sometimes banal, sometimes heart-rending reality is to detract from the exceptional quality of the work performed by these people who have dedicated their lives to doing "something beautiful for God". It is in their rationally incomprehensible capacity to see in the simplest of acts, in the most "distressing of disguises", something so beautiful that it triumphs over all natural revulsion, that their truly extraordinary quality lies. It is the turning of water into wine which demonstrates the miraculous, not the presentation of wine as wine in the first instance.

Nor, it must be stated and Mother Teresa has not hesitated to do so, is the need for a multitude of small miracles necessarily so far removed from the doorsteps of the affluent homes of the Western world. The physical poverty of parts of India and South America, for example, finds its relatively simple solution in a bowl of rice and a vitamin pill; the loneliness and the sense of being unwanted, which characterises the less tangible poverty of the West cries out even more hauntingly for that most miraculous but most demanding of all forces, namely love. Mother Teresa, the Missionary Sisters and Brothers of Charity and the many helpers known as her Co-Workers have responded to the cry of need which resounds from every corner of the world by doing "small things with great love" and the result has been what Pope Paul VI envisaged as early as 1964 as a "universal mission of love" – a mission, the full dimensions of which are yet to be appreciated.

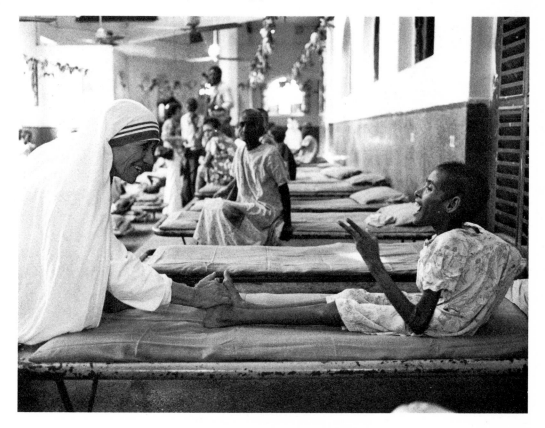

*"We can do no great things – only small things with great love."*

The awarding of the Nobel Peace Prize to Mother Teresa in 1979 focused the eyes of the world upon this mission and won her universal acclaim. She has been hailed as a saint by people of a variety of faiths and accordingly there have already been those who have attempted to raise her to a spiritual vantage point from which her life may bear little relevance to the lives of others. Yet this is completely contrary to her wishes. Without her faith Mother Teresa would be remarkable only for her ordinariness and she rejoices in this fact, for it is evidence of the power for which she and many others with her are but channels. If the miraculous has occurred it is because God has used her as an instrument of his own will; it is because, as she claims, she is "a little pencil in God's hand". So it is that the pencil or her personal life

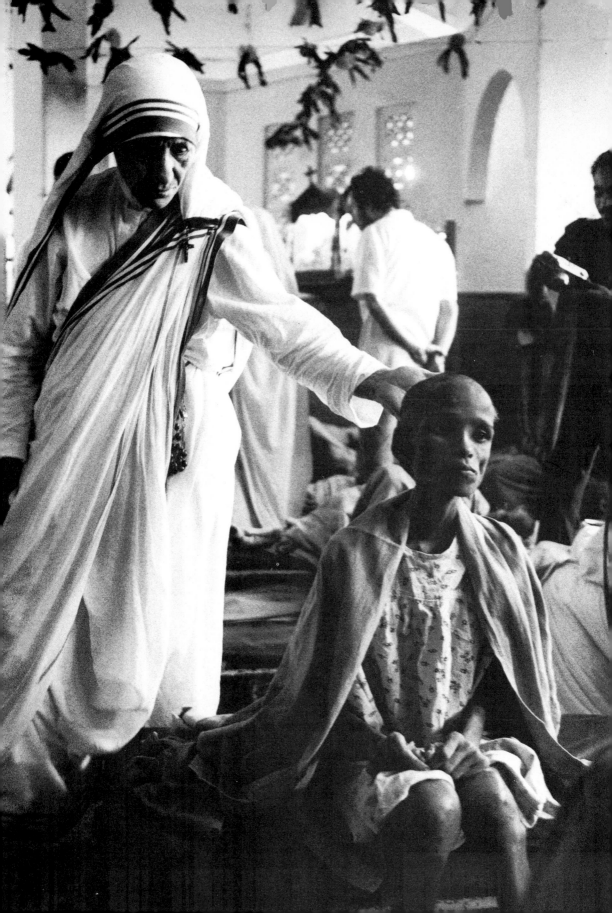

pales into insignificance. Like St Paul, she is fond of saying "Not I, but Christ who lives in me", and is at times disconcertingly reticent to talk about herself or her own feelings.

One interviewer in particular must remember with some embarrassment questioning Mother Teresa on television as to how she came to be doing such marvellous work. "Jesus" was the simple and uncompromising reply. The interviewer, who had evidently been expecting a considerably more prolonged and involved answer, was left floundering amongst his notes for the next question. Asked on another occasion how human suffering could ever be beautiful or bring joy, Mother Teresa replied with equal conviction, if a little more expansively: "Suffering does not, but Christ as seen in suffering does. We see Christ in two forms. We see him on the altar, under the appearance of bread and we see him in the slums, in the broken bodies of the forgotten people." To Mother Teresa it is Christ who is at his most vulnerable and who therefore cries out for even greater love in the horrifying sufferings of the poor, the lonely and the unwanted; it is God who acts through the otherwise insignificant instruments who offer themselves to give that love. Therefore we should not seek to turn from the "realities" of suffering – from the need which is sometimes so close and so lacking in drama that it passes unnoticed, nor should we seek to glorify the instruments themselves. Strangely, or perhaps not so strangely, this assertion, so sincerely expressed and so profoundly witnessed by Mother Teresa and by those who work with her, serves not only, as intended, to glorify their Lord, but also to emphasise the remarkable quality of his instruments.

---

*"When we cleanse the wounds of the poor, we are cleansing the wounds of Christ."*

CHAPTER ONE

# THE EARLY YEARS

Thither my own wings could not carry me,
But that a flash my understanding clove,
Whence its desire came to it suddenly.

High fantasy lost power and here broke off;
Yet, as a wheel moves smoothly, free from jars,
My will and my desire were turned by love,
The love that moves the sun and other stars.

DANTE: THE DIVINE COMEDY.

The tiny grey-eyed woman, now known to the world as Mother Teresa of Calcutta and referred to increasingly in India simply as "Mother", was born on the 27th August, 1910, in Skopje, Yugoslavia, of Albanian parents. Her name then was Agnes Gouxha Bojaxhiu. Her father was a grocer and Agnes was one of three children – two girls and a boy. She attended the local Government (Gimnazija) school and whilst there became a member of a Catholic association for children known as the Sodality of Mary. At the age of twelve, Agnes was already convinced that she had a vocation to the religious life. She was caught in a wave of enthusiasm for the missions and for the work of spreading the Gospel, an enthusiasm inspired by the writings of Pope Pius XI and endorsed by the institution of the Feast of Christ the King. It was at this time that the Yugoslav Jesuits had agreed to work in the Calcutta Archdiocese and one of the first to arrive there was sent to Kurseong. From there he wrote fervent and inspiring letters about the work of the missionaries among the poor and the sick, and the child Agnes responded with the unshakeable conviction that her calling was to become a missionary. Asked many years later about her family background, Mother Teresa's reply was characteristic: "It was a happy family. I had one brother and one sister, but I do

*"Let them look up and see no longer me – but only thou, Oh Lord."*

16

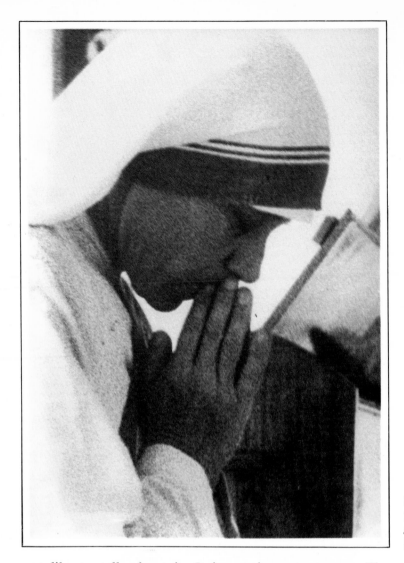

not like to talk about it. It is not important now. The important thing is to follow God's way, the way he leads us to do something beautiful for him." In complete submission to what she recognised unquestioningly as God's will, at the age of eighteen Agnes sought admission into the Congregation of Loreto nuns who worked in Bengal. She was sent first of all to the Loreto Abbey in Rathfarnham, Dublin, where she was to learn English. In a rather touching recollection a close friend of Mother Teresa tells of her admission that all she can remember of her stay in Dublin is the dining-room. To the young girl who spoke no English, removed from the backward but colourful life of Skopje to an austere Irish setting, food seems to have represented some small comfort.

From Dublin Agnes was sent to India to begin her novitiate in Darjeeling, where in the majesty and beauty of the Himalayas she saw little of the poverty she had expected. Her vocation to be a nun, however, was never put to question. Those searching later for some intimation of an internal dilemma were to be disappointed: "When I was eighteen I decided to leave my home and become a nun, and since then I've never doubted that I have done the right thing. It was the will of God. It was his choice." Obediently she accepted her role as a teacher of relatively affluent European children and some Indians at the Loreto Convent school in Darjeeling and on 24th March, 1931 took her first vows and with them, the name of Teresa, after St Thérèse of Lisieux, the French Carmelite nun who is the patroness of missionaries. Thérèse, known as the "Little Flower of Jesus", was a simple nun in an obscure convent who exemplified the "little way" – striving for goodness by executing the most humble of tasks. It is not difficult to imagine what attracted Mother Teresa, for whom holiness is the very simplest of duties, to this name.

The young Albanian nun, having completed her no-vitiate, was then attached to a High School for girls run by the Loreto Sisters at Entally, Calcutta. In an impressively spacious property the Sisters run a greatly respected English school for over five hundred girls, including a large number of orphans who are unable to pay any fees. St Mary's in the same grounds provides a separate institution where Bengali girls can be taught in their own language. It was here, in an oasis of well-kept buildings at Entally that Sister Teresa taught history and geography for seventeen years, taking her final vows on the 24th May, 1937 and eventually becoming principal of the school. She was also put in charge of the Daughters of St Anne, a diocesan Congregation of Indian nuns, who taught in the Bengali secondary school. At Entally there was a Sodality of the Blessed Virgin where the girls encountered the same thinking that had brought Sister Teresa to India. Members of the Sodality, together with some of the Hindu girls who belonged to a study club, regularly visited patients in the Nilratan Sackar hospital. They also went out into the slums of Motijhil to work among the poor. Sister Teresa heard their tragic accounts and saw the heart-rending poverty of many people in and around Calcutta for her room at the convent looked out upon vast expanses of squalor and poverty and the unattended sickness of Motijhil. "I knew where I belonged", she remembers, "but I didn't know how to get there".

In the period which preceded the partition of India, Calcutta suffered in a unique way from the fact that its population was almost evenly divided between the antagonistic Muslim and Hindu communities. In August 1946, when food supplies failed to reach her school, Mother Teresa herself went out into the streets to try to buy the necessary provisions. She found a city brought to a standstill by violence, its streets stamped with the marks of suffering and death. Increasingly she realised that her role was not within

*The poor foraged amongst the refuse in a city which could no longer supply adequate sanitation and waste disposal.*

the structures of organised education, aimed mainly at the middle classes, but among the "poorest of the poor" in slums such as Motijhil and Tiljala where old people lay dying on the pavements, foetuses were sniffed out by dogs from among the refuse and leprosy victims were driven away or invited to commit suicide by their own families.

On 10th September, 1946, a date now celebrated annually by Missionaries of Charity and Co-Workers throughout the world as "Inspiration Day", came what Mother Teresa describes as "the call within a call". In a train taking her to Darjeeling, the hill station in the Himalayas, she heard distinctly a second call from God. She had already been called to the religious life and to her there was never any question of abandoning it. Now she was being called to another form of work and service within that life. The message was quite clear: "I was to leave the convent and help the poor while living among them. It was an order. To fail it

*Refugees made their homes under scraps of old hessian and sacking.*

would have been to break the faith." Speaking of her own reluctance to communicate her personal feelings and reactions, Mother Teresa once confided: "The call of God to be a Missionary of Charity is the hidden treasure for me, for which I have sold all to purchase it. You remember in the Gospel, what the man did when he found the hidden treasure – he hid it. This is what I want to do for God." Somehow there is no probing into, no questioning so striking an intimacy with God. This is not the kind of relationship in which the Divine Will appears sometimes to be cheapened or reduced to the level of ensuring not man's spiritual but simply his material well-being. Mother Teresa lays every problem encountered, every requirement however apparently insignificant, at the feet of her Maker, but the overall perspective of "riches" that are not of this world is never lost.

Here the "treasure" consists of the requirement to leave even the basic comforts of the convent to become as one with the poorest of the poor; the only explanation offered is that "it is the will of God". Time and time again, in looking for the usual cobweb of reasons, motives and explanations for actions or events in the life of Mother Teresa, the response is quite simply "it is God's will". The statement is final; the authority is the ultimate one, and remarkably even the most cynical accept it – perhaps because it is spoken with such complete conviction, perhaps because it becomes impossible to doubt an authority, to the service of which the speaker's whole being has been so totally and so effectively surrendered.

Sister Teresa's response to the call in September 1946 was as always unhesitating. She explained her plan to work among the most needy to the ecclesiastical Head of the Archdiocese, Archbishop Périer, who gave her a sympathetic hearing and eventually his support. In February 1948, the General Superior of the Loreto nuns granted Mother Teresa permission to apply to the Roman Congregation for an indult of exclaustration, which would allow her to reside outside her convent, whilst remaining bound by her religious vows "in order to spend herself in the service of the poor and the needy in the slums of Calcutta, and to gather around her some companions ready to undertake the same work". The reply from the Congregation was received in August of the same year. Mother Teresa was granted permission to leave her convent initially for one year, for the purpose stated in her application. On the 16th August, 1948 she took off the religious habit she had worn as a Loreto nun, and put on the new habit of her future congregation: a cheap and simple white sari with a blue border, a small cross pinned to the left shoulder and open sandals on her feet. Leaving behind her the warmth and security of her religious house, she stepped out to spread the "fragrance of joy" over what Rudyard Kipling had referred to as the "Big Calcutta Stink".

To say that the response of this small woman was unhesitating is perhaps to suggest that it was undertaken without regret and with a blindness verging on naivety. Yet

Mother Teresa herself has admitted that the leaving of the convent was one of her most painful trials. "To leave Loreto was my greatest sacrifice, the most difficult thing I have ever done. It was much more difficult than to leave my family and country to enter religious life. Loreto, my spiritual training, my work meant everything to me." Nor was she blind to the hardships that awaited her. Her first move was characteristically practical. Recognising the need for some form of medical training, she travelled the 240 miles to Patna for a short course in nursing and dispensary work under the direction of Mother Dengal and her Medical Missionary Sisters. Mother Dengal, who had herself fought to obtain permission from the Holy See for her nuns to practice surgery and midwifery in their hospitals, gave Mother Teresa invaluable help, packing into her stay of only a few months, as much knowledge and experience as possible. She also gave her enthusiastic student advice which was to stand her in good stead in the years to come. Mother Teresa was determined to start a congregation whose members would lead the lives of India's poor. She and the girls whom she expected to join her would live, dress and eat like the poorest of the poor, whom they would tend, feed and clothe as the suffering Christ. The nuns' diet would consist solely of rice and salt, the humblest of Bengali diets. Mother Dengal very wisely insisted that such a diet would make the Sisters prey to the same diseases that afflicted the poor, and would therefore render them unable to work for Christ; Mother Teresa equally wisely and in all humility took this sound advice. She returned to Calcutta resolved that those who came to join her in her formidable task should receive the sustenance they required. In obedience they would eat no more but no less than necessary.

In December, 1948, Mother Teresa arrived back in Calcutta to be confronted by a city overwhelmed by human need. In 1947 India had gained its independence from the British but only after Pakistan had been divided off into a separate Muslim state. The panic-stricken flight of those Muslims and Hindus who suddenly found themselves in the territory of hostile religious groups was accompanied by

Overleaf: *In the midst of anguish and hostility – a channel of peace.*

savage riots in which many were killed and many more were wounded. Approximately eight million people fled from Pakistan to India. Bengal, because it contained both Hindus and Muslims, was divided into West Bengal which became a state in the Republic of India and East Bengal which formed the eastern wing of Pakistan. As a result, millions of Hindus fled from East Bengal and poured into the already over-populated new capital of West Bengal, i.e. Calcutta. The refugees, the majority of them penniless, jobless and hungry, squeezed into the "bustees". The buildings, which during the 19th century had been neat and relatively wholesome living quarters for workers in the factories, became synonymous with slums. Huts sprouted on the swampy tracts near the Hooghly river, city services failed, such drains as there were, clogged, so that in the monsoon months the streets were filled with water and excrement overflowing from the so-called "service privies" – little brick sheds with a platform above a two-foot-wide earthenware bowl at ground level, theor-etically emptied by municipal employees but frequently neglected. Disease ran rife and drinking water was in short supply. The city which under the British had been known as the "city of palaces", a predominantly pleasant and majestic home for the sahib and for those native Indians who made fortunes from the jute and rice that grows so plentifully, became increasingly the nightmare city of Nehru and Kipling's "City of Dreadful Night".

What could one woman alone achieve against such over-whelming odds? With hindsight, in the knowledge of what she has in fact achieved, the answer finds its triumphant echo in the words of St Francis de Sales: "One good woman can conquer a city". Even now, however, there are those who do not hesitate to point out, for example, that even the treat-ment of over 250,000 lepers or the finding of homes for nearly 3,000 abandoned children is but a drop in the ocean. Mother Teresa's answer makes a mockery of such reasoning: "I do not think the way you do. I never add up. I only sub-tract from the total dying. With children, one dollar saves a life. Could you say one dollar buys a life? No, but it is used to save it. So we use ourselves to save what we can. It is not the magnitude of our actions but the amount of love that is put into them that matters." In a letter to Co-workers through-out the world this gentle nun, whose very life spells love, writes modestly: "We can do no great things – only small ones with great love. He does not mind how much we do – what affects him is how much love we put into the work: Last year," she continues, "we had no sugar in Calcutta, and it was very difficult to get some for our abandoned children. A four year old Hindu boy heard this and hurried home and said to his parents: 'I shall eat no sugar for three days – I want to give mine to Mother Teresa' – how much sugar can a child of four eat? a small cup full – and the child said, 'I have gone without sugar for three days. This is for your children.' A small action but he had truly acted with great love." Love it may be replied, transforms small things and makes them great.

*Mother Teresa created her "Place of the Immaculate Heart" at the very centre of Hinduism, next to the Temple of Kali.*

Armed only with her faith and with the power to communicate unlimited compassion and hope in the most poignant of life's tragedies, it was with the intention of doing small things with great love that Mother Teresa began God's work among the poor of Calcutta. Living at first with the Little Sisters of the Poor, she began by opening a small school in Motijhil. The school was an open space among the huts, the children squatted in the dirt and Mother Teresa scratched the letters of the Bengali alphabet in the mud with a stick. Nevertheless, the handful of pupils who arrived on the first day doubled on the second, and increased steadily until the noise of the alphabet being repeated was a familiar sound in Motijhil. Mother Teresa had begun with five rupees (about 30p) given to her by her understanding Archbishop Périer but gradually, as people heard of what she was doing, they brought her money and they came to help. Some of the old girls and some of the teachers who had taught with her at the Loreto school joined her and together they taught the slum children not only the alphabet but also hygiene. Pupils were given milk at midday and awarded bars of soap as prizes. The love with which the work was carried out belied the nonsense of teaching the alphabet to waifs who would probably never read and hygiene to those who would never be able to buy soap.

By the spring of 1949 Mother Teresa was searching for a home nearer to the Motijhil. An entry in a diary which she kept for only a brief period contains one of the very few statements by her which comes anywhere near a complaint: "Today I learned a good lesson. The poverty of the poor must be so very hard for them. While looking for a home, I walked and walked until my arms and legs ached. I thought how much they must ache in body and in soul looking for a home, food, health." Even here personal suffering is turned into constructive insight into the suffering of others. Trudging from one scene of desolation to the next, despair is kept at bay by an implicit faith in the love of God: "Jesus has said that we are much more important to his father than the grass and the birds, and the flowers of the earth, and so if he takes such care of things like that . . . things, how much more would he take care of the life . . . of his own life in us." Her faith did not go unrewarded. In February, a Catholic priest, calling at the large ancestral house of Michael Gomes, an Indian teacher and a Roman Catholic, mentioned the work of Mother Teresa and the fact that she was looking for living quarters. The response from Michael Gomes' young daughter was immediate: "The rooms upstairs are empty. Mother could come here." Her father was equally insistent, refusing to accept any money for rent or food, and Mother Teresa eventually moved into one of the rooms on his upper floor, placed at her disposal, in the truest spirit of giving. Some years later in a letter addressed to "Mother's Co-Workers in England", Michael Gomes was to write with striking humility: "It is time I jotted down some notes on 'We received'. God sent Mother at the beginning of her mission to us and we *received* her. We did not give. Since then we have continued to receive and we are grateful." He goes on to

*"Shine through me that every soul I come in contact with, may feel thy presence."*

28

point out the tendency to lose sight of the fact that it is God who is at work in the remarkable achievements of a woman who has been prepared to follow her master to the last:

*"There are some who, like me, are awed and amazed by Mother's works and achievements, and that amazement does not go further. That Sunday's talk with Mother made me realise that we have to look at and be drawn by him (in the tabernacle), who works in and through Mother. Every work has had a simple and humble beginning. Her slum schools: she finds the need for one in an area, a spot is selected, a man is asked to clear the grass, and the ground is the blackboard, and a stick is used as chalk, the number of children increase, a passer-by is struck and he gives a table, and another gives a blackboard and so on."*

Naturally he does not mention that he too may well have been instrumental in furthering some indefinable plan of love.

By the time Mother Teresa moved into Michael Gomes' home in Creek Lane she had come to realise that she could not remain entirely dependent on voluntary or temporary help. Placing her trust in the Immaculate Heart of Mary, she prayed repeatedly: "I have no children as once you told your beloved Son 'they have no wine'." She insisted that her companions, her spiritual daughters, should not be mere lay-auxiliaries, but authentic religious, for "to be able to persevere in the work one needs great strength. A religious life alone can give this." Accordingly on 19th March, 1949, Subhasini Das, a Bengali girl who had been one of Mother Teresa's students at the Loreto Convent School, knocked on the door of Creek Lane to become her first postulant and the future Sister Agnes. Others soon followed. The first ten girls who arrived were all former pupils. One by one they heard God's call to surrender themselves entirely to the service of the poorest of the poor and together they went begging from door to door, taking the proceeds to whose who were starving in the streets, comforting the sick and the dying and teaching children the dignity of human life. All this was undertaken sometimes in the face of rejection and abuse but always in the conviction that they were responding to the words of Christ, "As you did it to one of the least of these my brethren, you did it to me".

Some years later a visitor to Calcutta watched a young novice cleansing a gaping wound in the body of a dying woman. The raw flesh was alive with squirming maggots and the novice, quite understandably, was removing them with a pair of tweezers held at arm's length. In an instant Mother Teresa, by this time in her late sixties, was by her side. Using a scalpel, she deftly began to cleanse the wound, her face close to the repulsive mass, apparently oblivious to the stench which was intensified by her probings. "You must understand that this is Jesus. We are cleansing the wounds of our Lord" was the instruction delivered to the young girl, who obediently took the scalpel and bent over her patient until her face was within inches of the putrid flesh. "If we didn't believe it was the body of Christ, we could never do it. No money could make us do this kind of work. The whole congregation is built on the direction 'Love one another as I have loved you'." "How else" comes the penetrating and haunting question, "could any Sister give up her home and family to do such dirty work?" The question defies all answers.

Over seven hundred years earlier, St Francis of Assisi wrote in his "Testament":

*"When I was still in sin, the mere sight of lepers was unbearable to me. But the Lord himself brought me among them and I tended them with all good will. By the time I left them, what had seemed to me so ugly had turned into sweetness in body and mind. So I waited a little while, and then said farewell to the world."*

It is not in the rationally explicable but in the mystery of faith and love that the power to see the beautiful in the abhorrent and the capacity to perform the "impossible", lies. Mother Teresa, recognising from the heart this fundamental principle, set about drawing up the constitution of a community composed, not as she repeatedly stresses, of social workers, but of those committed to a life of action based on prayer – a community of Sisters who are in the world but not of the world. "Jesus does not say 'hold fast to the world' but 'love one another as I have loved you'. You cannot love as he did without prayer. In whatever way you do that, and whatever religion is yours, pray together." Mother Teresa's aim is not to convert from one religion to another. It is, as she claims, to make a Christian a better Christian, a

Hindu a better Hindu, a Muslim a better Muslim and so on, but her directions on prayer are unquestionably emphatic – "A Sister who does not pray cannot remain with us – she might as well go. Through prayer you will believe and through belief you will love – through love you will serve."

A story drawn, not entirely inappropriately, from the traditions of Zen Buddhism recounts how the Emperor Wu of Liang once asked Dharma a question which had been greatly troubling him:

*"Ever since the beginning of my reign I have built so many temples, copied so many sacred books, and supported so many monks and nuns; what do you think my merit might be?"*

*"No merit whatever, sire!" was the blunt reply.*

*"How can this be?" demanded the Emperor, astonished.*

*"All these are inferior deeds", Dharma answered, "which would cause their author to be born in the heavens or on this earth again. They still show the traces of worldliness, they are like shadows following objects. Though they appear to actually exist, they are no more than mere non-entities. A truly meritorious action is full of pure wisdom and is perfect and mysterious, and its real nature is beyond the grasp of human intelligence. Such as this is not to be sought after by any purely worldly achievement."*

If the achievements of Mother Teresa and those who work with her appear not merely like "shadows following objects", but to be possessed instead of a "perfect and mysterious" quality it is perhaps because, in the words of Dharma, "their real nature is beyond the grasp of human intelligence". The constitution for the new Congregation of the Missionaries of Charity, drawn up almost exclusively by Mother Teresa herself and approved by the Pope on 7th October, 1950, demands acceptance not so much from the intellect with its endless facility for raising reasoned arguments and logical objections, but from the heart with its unique capacity for the spontaneous giving and receiving of love and for a wisdom and an understanding that at times defies intelligence.

*An understanding of the heart with its unique capacity for the spontaneous giving and receiving of love.*

Inscribed above the crucifix in every chapel of the Missionaries of Charity, be it in India, America or Australia,

33

are the two simple words: "I thirst". Mother Teresa's concept of the new congregation was based on the fundamental aim "to quench the thirst of Jesus Christ on the Cross" – the thirst which is the physical, symbolic expression of the spiritual cry for love and acceptance. The suffering Christ, himself the ultimate expression of sacrificial love, cries out for a response, a response which the Missionaries of Charity strive to provide in the observance of four vows, namely: to love Christ with undivided love in chastity, through the freedom of poverty, in total obedience and in wholehearted free service to the poorest of the poor. They must love unconditionally without seeking returns or results. They must love in chastity in a spirit of total surrender and they must love in poverty for poverty carries with it a state of non-attachment to material things and therefore a recognition of the greater riches of the Kingdom of Heaven. Poverty is an expression of love, it means total dependence on the will of God and it is a demonstration of solidarity with the poor who suffer misery and injustice – the evil which has resulted from sin. They must love too, in obedience, offering to God that thing which is particularly theirs because he gave it to them specifically – their free will. In obedience the Missionaries of Charity dedicate to their Lord their own will, thus identifying with the mystery of Christ, who saved men through his unconditional obedience to the will of the Father.

The fourth vow "to offer wholehearted free service to the poorest of the poor" is unique to the Missionaries of Charity. Its observance is an attempt to return the limitless love of God by freely and wholeheartedly loving him in the least of his brethren, with whom he has said he identifies. The "poorest of the poor" are the hungry, the thirsty, the naked, the homeless, the ignorant, the captives, the crippled, the leprosy sufferers, the alcoholics and drug addicts, the dying destitutes and the bereaved, the unloved, the abandoned, the outcasts and all those who are a burden to human society, who have lost all hope and faith in life. To these people and to Christ in them the Missionaries of Charity devote their prayers and their services, which in themselves become prayers, for in their daily work, however humble, however arduous, they live the Mass – touching Christ in the broken bodies of the poor, feeding him in the starving destitutes. At the same time they are encouraged to centre their life of

*message from Mother T. to sisters in Dacca*
*'If you die let me know'*

continuous prayer on the Eucharist, for here Christ in the form of bread offers himself to sustain.

The whole is potentially a complex fusion of the "seen" and the "unseen" in a labyrinth of mystical theology but Mother Teresa, with characteristic vision, expresses it with admirable simplicity: "This is all Jesus told us – 'love one another as I have loved you as the Father has loved me'. Father's love, Son's love, our love is but a 'giving' until it hurts. How great is his love for us. He makes himself the Bread of life to satisfy our hunger for love, and then he makes himself the hungry one – so that we can satisfy his love for us. Oh, the humility of God."

Mother Teresa dedicated her newly formed congregation to the Immaculate Heart of Mary in the conviction that it was born through the intercession of the Virgin. The Sisters strive to be like Mary for she of all created beings is in the most perfect likeness of God. Like the Mother of God they seek in all humility, to empty themselves of "self" in order that Christ may be present in them. To those who have come to associate the denial of the "lower self" with an air of severity however, one of the most remarkable characteristics of the many who endeavour to live in the spirit of Mother Teresa is their joy. "The poor", says Mother Teresa, "deserve not only service and dedication but also the joy that belongs to human love". A joyful heart is the natural result of a heart burning with love, and joy is also strength, for a person who is filled with joy preaches without preaching. With a lyricism which is enviably simple but unquestionably effective, she proclaims: "Joy is a net of love by which you can catch souls". The spirit of the Society is not only one of total surrender and loving trust but also one of cheerfulness.

In a pamphlet explaining the work carried out in this spirit throughout the world, a section is devoted to outlining what is required of those who wish to join the order:

*"Candidates who wish to join can be rich or poor and of any nationality. The qualities needed are that one be:*
*— Guided by the right intention.*
*— Desirous to serve the poor according to the Constitutions and to live and work as a Missionary of Charity.*
*— Healthy in body and mind and able to bear hardships.*
*— Able to acquire knowledge; of a cheerful disposition; and able to exercise sound judgement."*

It adds, very appealingly, that aspiring Missionaries of Charity should be:

*— "Possessed of a good sense of humour."*

The angel announcing the birth of Christ proclaimed "glad tidings of great joy". Joy as a distinguishing feature of the kingdom of Christ thus becomes a kind of spiritual obligation, to which humour, although arguably less sublime in nature, can serve as an aid. Those who have been close to Mother Teresa are fond of recounting amusing anecdotes about her, for she herself has an infectious sense of humour. A close friend recalls, for instance, the building of an extension in Calcutta: "Outside, between two main buildings, thirteen open-ended compartments were constructed in a row. Each was equipped with a tap so that the novices could wash properly. On the first morning that they were in use, the novices revelled in this new-found luxury but Mother Teresa was somewhat concerned that the compartments without doors afforded very little privacy. The young sisters were exposed to public view. On the following morning a parcel appeared mysteriously on the doorstep. Opening it, Mother Teresa found exactly thirteen shower-curtains, each one a perfect fit. "I shouldn't have worried," was the characteristic and amused response, "I should have known that the Lord was a better Mistress of Novices than me".

Laughter is a vital factor in those who have committed themselves to communicating love and therefore joy. The words "God bless you" uttered so frequently by the Missionaries of Charity are invariably accompanied by a radiant and delighted smile which somehow transmits itself even via a telephone line. Even in the earliest days in Creek Lane, where the adversities must have seemed almost insuperable and the future discouragingly uncertain, Michael Gomes recalls that his upper floor, by this time fully occupied, resounded with singing and with laughter. Members of the newly formed congregation began as they were to

*They treated elephantiasis and countless other diseases.*

continue. They tended to the weeping sores and emaciated limbs of the poor, they treated leprosy, cancer, venereal disease, elephantiasis and countless other diseases – all in the spirit of cheerfulness.

By the time the Missionary Sisters of Charity were made a diocesan congregation in 1950 it had become obvious that they must seek larger living quarters. In the house in Creek Lane they prayed fervently for somewhere to form a more permanent Mother house. Once again their prayers were answered. At about this time, Father Henry, a Roman Catholic priest who had ministered to the Bengali community since his arrival in India from Belgium in 1938, called on a wealthy Muslim gentleman who had decided to move to Pakistan. Father Henry, an enthusiastic supporter of Mother Teresa, interceded on her behalf and the Muslim gentleman who, it transpired, had been educated by the Jesuits, offered to sell his house for less than the price of the land on which it

*At the Mother house in Lower Circular Road, the Missionary Sisters of Charity welcome the Governor of Bengal and his wife.*

stood. The Archbishop of Calcutta approved the purchase and advanced the necessary money and the Missionaries of Charity moved into what was really three houses with a courtyard, at 54A Lower Circular Road in the very heart of Calcutta.

The street is a humming vortex of noisy pedestrians, trams and traffic but 54A Lower Circular Road – though now somewhat extended, has remained the Mother house of the Missionaries of Charity. The sounds of the city's congestion still mingle with their prayers. Here, despite their more extensive surroundings, the Sisters persisted in their life of poverty. Their only possessions consisted of two cheap cotton saris each, rough underwear, a pair of sandals, the crucifix they wear pinned to their left shoulder, a metal bucket for washing and a very thin palliasse to serve as a bed. The rule of poverty has remained unchanged over the years. "Our rigorous poverty is our safeguard", says Mother Teresa. "We do not want to do what other religious orders have done throughout history, and begin by serving the poor only to end up unconsciously serving the rich. In order to understand and help those who have nothing, we must live like them . . . The only difference is that these people are poor by birth, and we are poor by choice." So it is that, freed from the goods of this world, the Missionaries of Charity are able to move wherever Divine Providence, or Need dictates – with her mattress rolled up under her arm, a travelling Sister can carry all her possessions with her at short notice and with the minimum amount of disruption. A letter from some of the nuns in the Convent of Mercy in Australia, describes the arrival of the Missionaries of Charity in Bourke in 1969:

*"The first impression made on all those who welcomed the Sisters was the visible poverty of this new Congregation. Their habits, made of Indian cotton, cost one dollar each. Each Sister's belongings were rolled neatly in a thin mattress which was tied tightly by a rope. There were no suitcases whatever. But all was neat and orderly, very clean and very poor.*
*Cold winds marked the Sisters' first days in Bourke. Over their sari-like habits they wear about a third of a woollen blanket. Mother Teresa's looked like a man's singlet sewn together and darned well. We had tea together and then they*

*joined us in Chapel. Just as they do in India they wanted to kneel on the bare floor without support. They sit on the floor too – 'this saves time dusting furniture', Mother Teresa smilingly said. We helped them unroll their palliasses that they had brought with them. The Holy Father had given Mother four thousand of these mattresses for her nuns and for her poor. Each one would be about one fourth the thickness of our normal inner springs. They are short and the bed frames can be felt quite easily through them. As we unrolled each bundle we came to each Sister's personal belongings, neatly folded in each mattress. There was a feeling of awe as you can easily imagine. For the first time in our lives we had actually come up against voluntary and vowed poverty. We could not help remarking to each other how privileged we were to be here in Bourke for this outstanding experience."*

Remarkably the poverty which inspired such awe in Bourke, far from instilling a sense of undue deprivation in some of Mother's first Sisters, was insufficient to satisfy their desire to identify with the suffering poor. They wanted to reduce their own food consumption. Instead of eating four chappattis, might they not perhaps make do with only three chappattis per head for one of their meals. Mother Teresa, remembering the advice of Mother Dengal, insisted that they must feed well in order to resist disease. Some of the nuns in other congregations, and indeed in her own, suffered from tuberculosis. This must be combatted at all costs. The verdict on the Sister's request was settled with a prayer and a smile. They would receive not four, but five chappattis and they would eat them in obedience.

Gradually the first of Mother Teresa's Missionaries of Charity were joined by other helpers. Doctors, nurses, and other lay people worked with them on a voluntary basis and dispensaries were set up to cope with the sickness arising from malnutrition and overcrowding, a problem in the face of which the Calcutta Corporation, the governing body of the city, had already acknowledged itself to be virtually powerless. The starving destitutes, who made their pathetic homes on the platforms of the railway stations or simply slept and struggled for a pitiful existence in the streets, could not all be arrested or taken into care. The prisons were already overflowing and the hospitals filled to a dangerous bursting point. The Indian government, backed by international relief organisations, set up dispensaries and soup kitchens and managed to send some medicine and clothing into the slums, but the flow of destitute refugees from East Pakistan was seemingly interminable, the relief efforts were hopelessly inadequate and the starving and the disease-ridden lay dying on the pavements.

One wet day in 1954 a naked beggar boy of thirteen or fourteen stretched out his emaciated limbs to die by the roadside in a residential area. The occupant of a nearby house telephoned for an ambulance and the boy was taken to hospital, but being naked, he obviously did not have the necessary funds for treatment. The hospital, already overcrowded, rejected him, and his poor matchstick body was deposited back where it had been found. The young beggar boy died alone and untended in the gutter. The incident was, however, reported in the press. Public attention was drawn to the plight of this boy and the thousands of others like him, who could not even die with dignity.

Shortly afterwards Mother Teresa found a woman dying amongst the refuse, her body half eaten by rats and ants. She carried the woman in her arms to a nearby hospital – "they didn't want to take her", she recalls, "and I told them that I would stay at the hospital until they took her, and so to get rid of me I think they took the woman. And the same day I went to the municipality and I asked for a house." It was understandable that the hospitals should prefer to grant their limited number of free beds to patients who had some hope of recovery, rather than to those who were obviously and inevitably destined to die very soon of malnutrition or old age. Mother Teresa's request to the Municipal Authorities was an unusual one. She offered to take care of the starving, those dying in the streets – those for whom there was little if any likelihood of recovery. Some of the officials had, however, already noted the work of the Missionaries of Charity and their helpers in the slums. They realised also that in exchange for the gift of a "house", Mother Teresa was offering to salve the consciences of Calcutta's more socially-minded citizens. There would be no more criticism in the newspapers of a city which allowed some of its inhabitants to die without so much as a roof over their heads. They granted her, provisionally, a monthly sum of money and the use of the pilgrims' dormitories attached to the Kali Temple, an imposing building which rises high above congested streets, pilgrims' rest houses and "ghats" where the dead are cremated.

The Kalighat district is a popular place of pilgrimage for the Hindus, for it lies on the banks of the Hooghly River into which the sacred waters of the Ganges flow, and its temple is dedicated to the powerful Kali, the Goddess of Death and Fertility and consort of Siva. Hindu legend recounts how Kali's father made a sacrifice in order to guarantee the birth of his son but failed to include Siva, Kali's husband, in the ceremony. Kali, insulted by this omission, committed suicide and the grief-stricken Siva roamed the world, bearing his wife in his arms and threatening destruction wherever he went. The world was saved, however, by Vishnu, who hurled a discus at Kali's corpse. The scattered pieces of Kali fell to the ground sanctifying the places where they landed and most sacred of all was the spot where the toes of Kali's right foot came to rest, the Kalighat. The temple of Kali is thus a vital centre of worship and devotion for the Hindus and it is the wish of every devout Hindu in the city to be cremated in the Kalighat.

The official from the Corporation showed Mother Teresa two great rooms at right angles to each other and linked by an adjoining passage. They had once been used as a resting place for pilgrims who had completed their devotions to Kali. Mother Teresa's reaction was one of delight, for many reasons but particularly because, as she claimed: "this is a very famous Hindu temple and people used to come there and worship and rest so I thought that this would be the best place for our people to be able to rest before they went to heaven; so I accepted there and then. Within twenty-four hours the whole thing was arranged." With the remarkable speed, with which she embarks on all such undertakings, Mother Teresa created her Nirmal Hriday, a "Place of the Immaculate Heart" at the very centre of Hinduism and only a short distance from the walls of a temple regularly daubed with the blood of sacrificial sheep and goats. Her intention was not, as some at first suggested, to convert Hindus to Christianity, to offer them shelter in exchange for acceptance of the Christian faith, but to allow them to die according to what is written in the book: "be it written according to the

Hindu, or Muslim or Buddhist, or Catholic, or Protestant, or any other religious faith". The sick and the destitute, the beggar picked up from the streets, the leper rejected by his family, the dying man refused admittance to a hospital – all are taken in, fed, washed and given a place to rest. Those who can be treated are given whatever medical attention is possible; those who are beyond treatment are given the

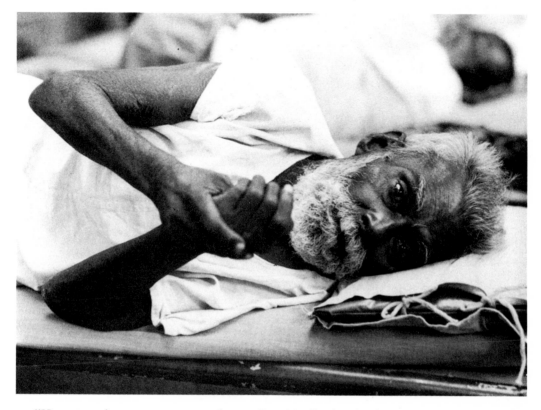

*"How many times we have picked people up from the street who have lived like animals and long to die like angels."*

opportunity to die with dignity, having received the rituals of their faith; for Hindus, water from the Ganges on their lips; for Muslims, readings from the Koran; for the rare Christian, the last rites. To Mother Teresa and those who assist her, the fact that only about half of the thousands who have now been taken into the "Nirmal Hridays" throughout the world, have been restored to health, is not the all-important factor.

What is equally important is the fact that those who have died, have been able to do so "beautifully". The apparent incongruity of the adverb inevitably provokes the question, "What is a beautiful death?" "A beautiful death is for people who lived like animals, to die like angels – loved and

43

wanted." It is for one old man who had never slept in a bed in his life to clutch the side of his simple bed frame and proclaim with a radiant smile, "Now, I can die like a human being". It is to catch a glimpse of the God who transcends all differences in religious teaching and to die in the recognition of his love and the acceptance of his will.

*At the Eucharistic Congress in Philadelphia Mother Teresa joins in prayer with the Brazilian Archbishop, Dom Helder Camara.*

During a visit to Philadelphia for the Eucharistic Congress of 1977, Mother Teresa was approached by a woman carrying a tiny baby and asked to pray that the child would not die. "She is only ten weeks old and she has to have a heart operation", the mother pleaded. A friend explained that the baby was mongoloid and would have to be taken care of for the rest of her life, even if she survived the operation. Yet the mother cried repeatedly: "I want my baby to live. I want this child. Pray that she will live." Tears streamed down the woman's face as Mother Teresa touched the pale cheek of her sick child but remarkably the tears ceased to flow as the older woman spoke: "God has given you this great gift of life. If he wants you to give the gift back to him, give it to him willingly, with love." Mother Teresa teaches and embodies an acceptance of the will of God which transcends what many would consider natural human reactions, emotions and abilities. So effective is her own example that it evokes in many others – even in the most unlikely quarters – a response which she would doubtless describe as "beautiful". This is not to suggest that she and her helpers have not encountered bitterness, resentment, or criticism but to counterbalance all this, there is always a "giving", be it great, or simply small with great love, which is indeed "beautiful" and which defies denial of the presence of Christ in man.

In the early days of Nirmal Hriday there was a considerable amount of hostility towards the foreign lady and her companions who were considered to be encroaching on Hindu territory. Stones were thrown at the Missionaries of Charity as they tried to carry the sick into their refuge of peace. Gradually, however, the pre-eminence of charity above all things commanded recognition. Those who came to criticise watched as the Missionaries of Charity applied potassium permanganate to the maggot-ridden wounds of the dying; they learned how Mother Teresa had lifted a young priest, who had served in the Kali Temple, from a pool of his own vomit and filth, and brought him to be nursed and eventually to die in peace. The result was something indisputably "beautiful". The resentment and the menaces stopped, Hindu pilgrims paused en route to the temple to bring gifts to those who offered unconditional love, and in the course of time the small statue of the Virgin Mary, which stood in the corner of one of the two great rooms, was adorned with a crown made from the golden nose rings of the Indian women who died there. As Mother Teresa put it, "Those who had nothing have given a crown to the Mother of God".

# CHAPTER TWO

## SHISHU BHAVAN:
## A HOME FOR CHILDREN

# I know of nothing sadder Than the lack-lustre eyes in a child's face.

MICHEL QUOIST

The work with children which had begun so humbly in an expanse of mud among the huts of Motijhil was growing. It grew in an attempt to achieve the impossible – in an effort to provide unlimited love and care for the apparently equally unlimited number of unwanted children who must otherwise fend for themselves or die on the streets of Calcutta. Orphans, sick, crippled or mentally handi-capped children whose parents found themselves unable to support them, children whose mothers had died in Nirmal Hriday, babies born of unmarried mothers who would never be accepted back into their families – all to Mother Teresa and the Missionaries of Charity, represented the infant Christ for whom a Nazareth must be provided. Other charities were already at work in this field but the need was still overwhelmingly great and so it was that in 1955, Shishu Bhavan, the first of what was to become a whole series of children's homes, was opened.

Shishu Bhavan, Calcutta, is a very ordinary two-storeyed building with a large courtyard, only a few hundred yards from the Mother House in Lower Circular Road, but in 1955 it became a refuge of exceptional love for crippled and
*They tended to children whose eyes, prematurely old, reflected some unspoken, tragic wisdom.* unwanted babies and children, some of whom were found in dustbins and drains or simply abandoned on the city railway platforms. Nearly all were suffering from acute malnutrition and tuberculosis; all were crying out for love. Each day

My dear Mark
Thank you
for your gift.
Love Jesus and
Mary God bless
you & your Sister
and little Baby
M. Teresa.

*A letter written in extra-large handwriting for the benefit of one small boy has become a treasured memento.*

children were discovered and brought to the home by the Missionary Sisters and, perhaps even more tragically, by parents who were forced to accept their own inability to feed and support their families. Gradually the word spread — children were sent to Shishu Bhavan by the police, by social workers, by doctors and eventually by hospitals. Some of the babies were so tiny that their very survival spoke only of the miraculous; some of the older children with emaciated limbs, distended stomachs and eyes which, prematurely old, reflected some unspoken tragic wisdom, were, inevitably, permanently scarred by their experiences. Yet no child was ever refused a home. God in his boundless love would provide, even if it meant that the babies slept three or more to a cot or were coaxed into life in a box heated by a simple light bulb.

Mother Teresa's approach to caring for these unwanted waifs has always been an essentially practical one. Whenever possible the sick must be restored to health and those capable of learning must be given some form of education or training to equip them for the future. A letter from one Sister working in the home provides some insight into its achievements: –

*"A tremendous transformation takes place in a normal child over the first year. First there is a physical change, especially an increase in weight; the shy ones lose their shyness – some only look for attention – all crave for love. As the children grow in strength we are able to send them to proper schools. A generous Hindu lady of Calcutta, Mrs Romola Sinha sponsored the first ten children for ten years. Without fees, no school in Calcutta or elsewhere will accept the children, though some reduction is available. We have to pay fees for all our children who are boarding in schools. As our children are already unfortunate enough to have no parents or to have been abandoned by them, we would like at least to give them a good education. We ourselves run slum schools which are not recognised by the Government. Those who are not clever enough to pursue regular studies are taught some handicraft such as needlework for the girls, etc., and money is given to them as a dowry when they get married. Some children are adopted. As the children grow up, it is heart-warming to realise that although they have been taken from the slums, often abandoned, they need now never, with God's help, return there."*

The system of sponsorship initiated by Mrs Sinha guaranteed the future of individual children for some years. A baby sponsored by an Indian "parent" or, in the years that would follow, by "parents" throughout the world, would be provided with a regular sum of money which would be placed in a bank account until he reached school age and then used to finance his schooling. Later, in 1975 this system of individual sponsorship would be replaced by a general World Child Welfare Fund which would share any financial assistance fairly between all of the thousands of children who were by this time in the care of the Missionaries of Charity.

Whatever the method of providing for them, however, Mother Teresa, who herself became an Indian citizen in 1948, was ever conscious of the need to equip these children for the requirements of Indian society. Some of the youngsters who came to Shishu Bhavan were returned to their parents once their strength and health had been restored. Others were adopted by parents who were always carefully chosen – Hindu children by Hindu parents, Christian children by Christian parents and so on. Some went to families in other parts of the world, wherever a secure and stable future could be guaranteed. For those who remained in her charge, however, Mother Teresa endeavoured, in accordance with Indian custom, to arrange marriages. The social backgrounds of the majority of girls in her care would not make such a task an easy undertaking but it was ensured at least, that each girl had a dowry of a new sari, a few trinkets and a wedding ring. A remarkable story is told of one young Hindu girl who was approaching marriageable age. One of the Sisters was sent, as is customary, to a marriage broker, who duly arranged for the girl to marry a policeman. Mother Teresa, whose own faith is profoundly and unshakeably rooted in the teachings of the Roman Catholic Church, provided the dowry and herself gave the bride away at the marriage ceremony. Later, in truly Hindu fashion, she joyfully welcomed the girl and her husband back into the bride's old home, Shishu Bhavan.

Tales such as this belie the natural assumption that the tragedy of being unloved, homeless and suffering from all the heart-breaking effects of poverty, must pervade the atmosphere of Shishu Bhavan – and rightly so, for despite the sorrowful circumstances which have made its existence necessary, the overall impression in the home is one of smiling young faces inviting attention and love. Naturally there are those for whom the care offered by the Missionaries of Charity comes too late. For all those babies who survive the shock of premature birth, attempted abortion or simply of being unwanted, to become healthy, gurgling children, there are always those who die within an hour of arrival. Mother Teresa's response moves easily from the realms of the unquestionably practical to those of unqualified love:

"I don't care what people say about the death rate. Even if they die an hour later we must let them come. These babies must not die uncared for and unloved, because even a tiny baby can feel." If they are to die then they must do so "beautifully". They must not do so without experiencing, if only for the most fleeting of instants, all the love it is within her power to give.

*"Every child is the infant Christ."*

There have been many who have suggested that the solution to the problem of India's rapidly increasing population lies in sterilisation or abortion. To Mother Teresa such suggestions are utterly abhorrent and incomprehensible. To her every child is the infant Christ; its destruction by abortion must be seen inescapably as a crucifixion. In her Nobel lecture on 11th December, 1979, much to the discomfiture of many present, she condemned the attitude of many people in the West towards what she described as the "murder of a child by its mother":

"I feel the great destroyer of peace today is abortion, because it is a direct war, a direct killing, direct murder by the mother herself. And we read in the scripture, for God says very clearly, 'Even if a mother could forget her child, I will

51

not forget you; I have curved you in the palm of my hand.' We are curved in the hand of God. What strikes me most is the beginning of that sentence, that even if a mother *could* forget (and this is something seen as impossible) – even if she could forget, I will not forget you."

Mother Teresa does not approve of government sterilisation programmes in India – even for leprosy victims, despite the fact that they frequently infect their children:

"A child is their only joy in life. The rich have so many other things. If you remove a child from the home of the poor, or from those with leprosy, who is going to smile at them and help them to get better?" Her reasoning is the logic of love. "Unrealistic" perhaps at first to thinking conditioned by the Western worship of convenience and expediency but entirely consistent with that same principle of infinite compassion, of "loving until it hurts" the Christ present in every man, that has induced the Missionaries of Charity and the Co-Workers to tread where others have feared to go, to tend the nauseating wounds of the leper or to work at great personal risk among the victims of violence in places such as Amman, Bangladesh or Belfast. The "beautiful" is to be found in the most unexpected places: "Very often we see a leper woman who is scarcely able even to walk, walking for miles, just to come to Sister to make sure that her child is alright. She has spotted the sign of leprosy in the child so she comes walking. . . . all the way walking. We had the wonderful case of a woman who scarcely had any feet to walk on and she had walked more than six miles. And she came with this baby in her arms and said 'Sister, see, my child also has leprosy.' She had seen a spot. The Sister examined the child and took the smear but it was not leprosy, and the woman, she felt so happy that her child didn't have leprosy that she took the child and she walked all the way back – she didn't even stop to rest or anything. That's a very beautiful thing." Who are we then to determine that the potentially beautiful, the simple, unassuming evidence of the presence of Christ in each and every man is merely one more dispensable commodity? Nor is the suggestion that we should place our trust in the infinite love of God an attempt to shelve personal responsibility for no one could have a greater practical commitment to the well-being of the poor, the suffering and the unloved.

In her Nobel lecture Mother Teresa went on to announce:

"We are fighting abortion by adoption. We have saved thousands of lives. We have sent word to all the clinics, to the hospitals and police stations: 'please do not destroy the child; we will take the child'. So every hour of the day and night there is always somebody – we have quite a number of unwedded mothers – to tell them 'come, we will take care of you, we will take the child from you, and we will find it a home'. We have a tremendous demand from families who have no children, which is the blessing of God for us. Also, we are doing another thing which is very beautiful. We are teaching our beggars, our leprosy patients, our slum dwellers, our people of the street, natural family planning. In Calcutta alone in six years we have had 61,273 less children from the families who would have had them because they practise this natural way of abstaining, or self-control, out of love for each other. We teach them the temperature method which is very beautiful and very simple and our poor people understand."

The annual report on the work of the Missionary Sisters of Charity – for the year 1979 includes the eye-catching entry:

Natural Family Planning Centres: 161
Number of Cases: 194,344

At these centres only the rhythm method or what Mother Teresa rather charmingly describes as "Holy Family Planning" is taught. As an orthodox Roman Catholic, it may be suggested, she could not act in any other way, but even disregarding such "metaphysical considerations" the impracticality and, in some instances, danger, of teaching some alternative methods to people who cannot always be properly supervised and whose grasp of such matters may be somewhat limited, is quite considerable. A story concerning one woman who attended one of the family planning centres in Calcutta illustrates that even "Holy Family Planning" has its limitations. The woman, who had already given birth to a number of children, wished to avoid becoming pregnant again, and was accordingly given instruction in the rhythm method and a string of beads of various colours to help keep a record of the safe period. Some time later she returned to the clinic somewhat confused as to why she was once again pregnant. "I hung the beads round the neck of Kali", she protested, "and still I am pregnant". Needless to say, despite a success rate which is impressive, the homes for abandoned children are still bursting at the seams.

Shishu Bhavan, Calcutta, is now the largest work centre of the Missionaries of Charity, a hive of constant activity, always teeming with children and always the focal point of an apparently endless queue of leaden footed people waiting for food or medicine. Mother Teresa recalls how in December 1966 some little boys were caught stealing: "Instead of handing them over to the police, the people brought them to me. And I asked the children 'But why do you have to do this? Why do you have to do wrong? You are so small.' And they said: 'Every day between 4.30 and 7 in the evening some big people come and teach us how to steal and how to do the wrong thing'. Then I thought it would be very nice if we could do something for these children to keep them away from those parts at that time. We started a high school for these street children: boys and girls – to prevent them from being in the streets during those hours. So we are using a school – they close school at half past three. We take over at four until half past seven and there is a Hindu gentleman, well to do, and I told him about the school and he said, 'Mother, I will finance the school in memory of my wife'. Wherever and whatever the need, with God's help it must be met." This is one of the principles upon which Mother Teresa and the Missionaries of Charity base their work and this is the principle which ensured the expansion of the role of Shishu Bhavan, for here now, in addition to the care provided for children, free treatment and medication is given to hundreds of sick adults each week. From here cooked food or "kitcherie" is distributed daily to the hungry, and from here also an ambulance donated by Pope Paul VI sets out each morning to distribute rations and to carry helpers and medicines to no less than eight leprosy centres each week, giving free treatment to over 13,000 victims of the disease.

---

*Prince Charles interrupts his tour of India in 1980 to meet children in the care of the Missionaries of Charity.*

# CHAPTER THREE

# SHANTI NAGAR:
# A SMALL TOWN FOR THOSE
# WHOM NO-ONE WANTS

And a leper came to him
beseeching him, and kneeling said to him,
"if you will, you can make me clean".
Moved with pity, he stretched out his hand
and touched him and said to him,
"I will; be clean".
And immediately the leprosy left him,
and he was made clean.

MARK 1:40

Estimates of the number of leprosy sufferers in the world today vary considerably between seven and fifteen million. Suffice it to say, therefore, that the disease which declined with astonishing rapidity in the Europe of the 15th and 16th centuries still has a very high incidence in areas such as parts of South America, Africa, China and India. Leprosy does not kill. Nor is every case of leprosy infective. In India it is estimated that about eighty per cent of the two to three million cases are non-infective and do not represent a public health problem. Of the infective cases, it has been found that they are only infrequently a threat to well fed adults, for this most crippling of all diseases tends only to be contracted by susceptible people (more particularly children) who come into close daily contact with an infectious case. Where there is great poverty, cramped living conditions and malnutrition the disease is inevitably rife and may spread with relative ease. In and around Calcutta therefore, where poor nutrition, overcrowding and inadequate medical attention determines the tragic struggle for survival of so many, leprosy constitutes a serious problem. More difficult than the treatment of the actual symptoms of the disease, however, is the combating of the irrational fears and myths associated with it. A sufferer, fearing the ostracism, unemployment and rejection which frequently accompanies the revelation that he is a leper, will conceal the illness until it has reached its more advanced stages and even then may well be reluctant to undergo treatment in the alien world of a hospital far removed from his home and family. Sadly, that family may ultimately reject him anyway. The following extract which dates, not from biblical times, not from the Middle Ages, but from September 1977, provides a pitiful insight into the feelings of a young Korean girl who contracted the disease at the age of seven:

*"A leper has to be got rid of fast. Even those who love you tell you to kill yourself. It is the best way out for everybody. The owner of the one room who let my poor parents rent sleeping space said I had to go, or else the whole family would have to go. Where could they go? My parents and brothers and sisters then got cruel with me. My parents had to be cruel to me to live themselves. They had to throw me out. Everyone I met kept telling me to do away with myself. My parents came and took me to a deep river, embraced me and hugged me and cried goodbye: my father in his numb way, my mother with streams of tears. After they had gone, I cried until I cried myself dry. The sun went down behind the mountain. I knew I had to, but I still couldn't jump in the river to die. And though I knew that way for me was the only way for my parents to live – and I only seven years – I couldn't go into the river even to stop the terrible pain of hunger in my belly. There was no hope, but I lived here and there, hiding in the fields.*
*In despair I came back home shivering to my parents. My parents promised to die with me. All of us would go out together and lie down on the railway track. And they were embracing me and crying about it when a person we barely knew said he would take me and get me into a leper settlement, and he did and my parents did not have to die after all. I found out later that this person who saved my parents' life and mine was a Catholic believer."*

It was to meet this kind of heart-rending need that the Missionaries of Charity, from their very earliest days as a

Congregation, had run a leper asylum at Gobra on the outskirts of Calcutta. It so happened, however, that plans for the development of Calcutta included the district of Gobra. The houses and large compound occupied by the one hundred and fifty or so lepers, who would otherwise have been driven to scavenge for a wretched existence on the city's rubbish tips, were to be expropriated and incorporated into the new development. The healthy citizens of Calcutta would never accept accommodation in close proximity to an area which they considered to be infected by a disease they so abhorred. Mother Teresa, appealing to the authorities, managed to persuade them not to evacuate the colony until some alternative accommodation could be found for them. She was offered a place in Bankura district but with some indignation she pointed out that the area proposed lacked even the most fundamental necessity for the well-being of the leprosy patients – an adequate water supply. The tragic plight of the lepers who were still it seemed, the "unclean" of biblical times or of mediaeval Europe, impressed itself even more deeply upon her and she became an active campaigner on their behalf. A Leprosy Fund and a Leprosy Day were started. On the collection boxes were inscribed the simple but incisive words: "Touch a leper with your compassion". The invitation was not merely to give at a distance from a surfeit of wealth but rather to reach out in love to the Christ whose maimed hands and feet could feel no pain and were therefore susceptible to every conceivable form of injury. Remarkably the people of Calcutta responded with overwhelming generosity.

Someone once remarked somewhat rashly to Mother Teresa that he would not help or touch a leper for a thousand pounds. "Neither would I", was the instant reply "but I would willingly tend him for the love of God". The conviction of Mother Teresa and her helpers was absolute but the practice of that conviction amongst those whose vision was clouded by fear and superstition was not always easy. Mrs Ann Blaikie, a close friend of Mother Teresa and the future International Chairman of the Co-Workers, remembers visiting a plot of land between two railway lines where Mother Teresa wanted to build a leper clinic. The local Councillor who was present at the time asked the crowd of villagers who had inevitably gathered to witness their arrival, whether they wanted a leper clinic. The response was unmistakeably hostile. "The villagers picked up stones and started to hurl them at us. We had to run for the car. 'Oh dear', said Mother Teresa 'I don't think God wants us to have a leper clinic here. We shall pray for two months and see what He does want'." In the course of the next two months, 10,000 rupees were given to Mother Teresa by Philips Electric Light Company. Dr Sen, a Hindu specialist in leprosy at the Carmichael Hospital for Tropical Diseases, retired from his official post and offered the rest of his working life to Mother Teresa and an ambulance was sent out to her from America. The first of Mother Teresa's mobile leprosy clinics was born.

*Ambulances carrying medicaments to those areas where they were most needed could arrest the disease and sometimes cure it.*

Leper asylums were not enough. A leprosarium could look after two or three hundred patients but the total number of sufferers in India at that time was in excess of two million. Mobile leprosy clinics on the other hand, could provide a much needed approach to the masses. The discovery of the Sulphone drug, Dapsone or D.D.S., meant that patients could be treated in their own homes. Ambulances carrying this and other medicaments to those areas where they were most needed could arrest the disease and in some cases cure it and, what was of vital importance to Mother Teresa, they could do so without removing the patient from his family, his essential source of love, or from his employment, the mainspring of his dignity. In September, 1957, Mother Teresa's first mobile leprosy clinic was opened by Archbishop Périer at Shishu Bhavan on Lower Circular Road. Work started on 1st November of that year and by the following January six hundred lepers were attending regularly. The work spread and more centres were opened, the ambulance visiting each centre once a week. By 1958 the work of the mobile clinic had been recognised at least by one witness as verging on the miraculous:

"Here in Howrah, I saw an experiment in mercy – a miracle it would have been called in a less cynical age. Into the clearing drove an ambulance and in minutes people crowded about its open doors. And no ordinary people these. Beyond the lines of abysmal poverty and under-nourishment etched upon their faces, below the tell-tale marks of frustration and harsh treatment were the scars of a deeper distress – leprosy."

Wherever there were large concentrations of lepers, it was Mother Teresa's hope to establish "static all-weather

*The opening of the Leprosy Dispensary at Titagarh.*

dispensaries". It goes almost without saying, that the first of these was constructed within a very short period of time. In March, 1959 Mrs Blaikie, on behalf of Mother Teresa, who was present but ever reticent to speak in public, thanked the Volkart Foundation Trust for financing the building of a Leprosy Dispensary at Titagarh, the Titagarh Municipal Council for making the necessary land available and the Speaker of the West Bengal Assembly for opening it. The

*Shanti Nagar became a small town for those whom no one wanted.*

speech was given in the presence of what one reporter described succinctly as the "social élite". Also listening if not understanding were 240 Titagarh lepers sitting in rows, awaiting a promised feed and a handout of blankets. After the speech, buns, biscuits, oranges and blankets were distributed amongst them. "A crippled woman peeled an orange to feed her child. A man fumbled with fingerless hands to offer cake to a pariah puppy cradled in his lap" –

61

and all this took place against the backcloth of the new clinic, blessed by the Archbishop of Calcutta, its paint new smelling and its promise a bright beacon on the very edge of bustee land.

Such is poverty that no sooner had the Titagarh clinic opened than the Municipal Chairman was compelled to beg Mother Teresa to start another nearby "or else every leper within miles will come crowding to Titagarh". There were at the time 30,000 known lepers in Calcutta and Mother Teresa was already treating 1,136 of them. "So wonderful is the way of God," was her only comment, "we will eventually get them all".

Treating the lepers involved not only the dispensing of Sulphone drugs, the tending of subsidiary ailments and the distribution of free milk and rice; it involved above all, the restoration of the dignity and confidence of the patients whose sense of identity had frequently been undermined by fear.

For this reason those who attended the clinics were encouraged wherever possible, to provide for their own needs. Those who were able to use their hands were shown how to make shoes from foam rubber cuttings and old rubber tyres for feet that were often all too vulnerable. They wove their own bandage cloth, made their own clothes and even managed some carpentry. So much could be achieved, particularly if the disease was caught in its early stages. "The Sisters go out spotting the disease," Mother Teresa confided to an interviewer some years after the opening of Titagarh. "You see, if they come in time . . . what we call young cases . . . as soon as they discover that they have a spot or something, then in a year or two they can be completely cured and nobody will know that they have had the disease. In India, the idea is once a leper — a leper for life. Very often it happens there are broken homes, broken lives. Among our disfigured beggars there are people who have been somebody in life. Last Christmas we had a party for all our lepers. Every leper was given a parcel of food and clothes and things like that. At every centre we have made them choose their own leader, and they have their own council, so that we can deal with them when we have so many thousands in a group. Each leader is responsible for their own group. One gentleman once got up to thank the Sisters for what they had done for him and then he said: 'Some years back I was a very big man and I was working in offices in a large building; (as a government official) and I had air-conditioning and people to answer me at every call. I had people bowing to me when I used to come out of my office and I had a big family. But at once when they discovered I was a leper all that went. There was no more air-conditioning, no fans, no home, no family – only these young Sisters who wanted me and who are my people now.' That", Mother Teresa continued, "is the story of most of our beggars. So we are hoping that by going to them . . . you see when we get a patient, we go to the family and examine them and try to prevent the others from getting it. That is from the positive cases; from the negative cases they won't catch it anyway. Now the Government has given us thirty-four acres of land and we are hoping to make that into a training and rehabilitation centre for our leprosy families. And the Holy Father gave a car, and we raffled that car, and with the money we have started."

*Pope Paul VI pauses to talk to a group of young people during his visit to India in 1964.*

The car to which Mother Teresa was referring, was a splendid white Lincoln Continental which had been provided for the use of Pope Paul VI during his visit to India in 1964 and which on his departure, he chose to give to her work. Mother Teresa treated no-one to the incongruous vision of a slight figure dressed as one of the poorest of the poor, sparing her worn sandals by riding the streets of Calcutta in a ceremonial limousine. Instead she very

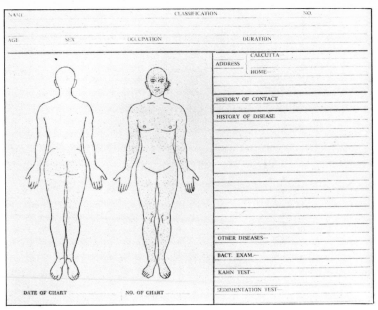

*The poignant needs of the lepers were met with every available means:* left: *a simple chart used to record a patient's condition,* below: *the invitation to reach out in love.*

shrewdly raffled it, earning many times more in this way than would have been gained by an outright sale. The proceeds were put towards a project which had already been started from funds raised by German children singing on the Feast of the Three Kings – one of Mother Teresa's most cherished dreams – a place where lepers could live and die with dignity, where they could work gainfully and lead constructive lives approaching the "normality" so frequently taken for granted. To the thirty or so dwellings already under construction, the Pope's gift added a hospital and a contribution from the Papal Propagation of the Faith in Germany provided a convent and chapel. Shanti Nagar, "The Place of Peace" and the fulfilment of a dream, began to form a green oasis in an expanse of dust approximately six motoring hours from the heart of Calcutta.

A well was constructed, ponds were stocked with fish, and banana and palm trees were planted several years before the first leper families moved in. The idea was to make the inhabitants self-sufficient. The first arrivals learnt how to make bricks and so helped to build homes for those who were yet to come. Despite, in some cases, the handicap of sadly maimed limbs, the villagers looked after their own poultry and cattle, grew their own rice and tilled their own paddy fields. They made baskets to be sold for use in the coal mines and even started a printing press, and all this in a spirit of dignity and independence and within the reassuring context of their own family life. Shanti Nagar was independent of the Sisters, in the sense that it was run on the Indian Panchayat system of village elders, elected from among the inhabitants themselves, and under this system it flourished. By 1971 the Sister in charge at Shanti Nagar was able to write with justifiable optimism to those supporting the venture:

"Our patients were not allowed to purchase anything in the grocer's shop, so I had to start a small shop for their needs. Now one of the patients is running it, but he does not like to take the full responsibility of the running. He has a kind of fear that he may lose. I had in the end to accept that job also. Anyhow the patients are greatly benefitting from it, as we are running it on a co-operative basis. Also one is having a tea stall, another a tailoring shop. I give him second-hand clothes and he makes new ones of them and sells them – the proceeds go to him as he has his family with him. Now we have started to construct the second group of housing units, for another hundred patients and their families. We need lots of big prayers from all of you. The money will come if we can do the work according to the will of our good God."

Mother Teresa's original plan for Shanti Nagar envisaged the settling of about four hundred families who must all somehow be accommodated in inexpensive, easily maintained but attractive huts and who must all be given the appropriate medical treatment. Her answers to queries about the availability of resources or of surgical skills were, as always, that God would provide and remarkably God appears to have done precisely that. One doctor at the Leprosy Study Centre in London remembers with some amusement a telephone call apparently from out of the blue:

"I'm speaking on behalf of Mother Teresa", said the voice on the telephone. "Can you tell me where I can buy a million tablets of dapsone?"

I could and I told her, and I added for good measure that I should like to know that they would be given to the right people at the right dose for the right disease.

Almost inevitably the doctor in question found himself in India with the Missionaries of Charity helping to "add a modicum of medical knowledge to their Christian compassion, a smattering of diagnosis and treatment to their love and concern". The Sister in charge is herself qualified as a doctor and she has passed on her surgical skills to her assistants, many of whom are arrested lepers.

Today Shanti Nagar is approached via an avenue of lush flowering trees. In contrast to the bare simplicity of the Mother house in Lower Circular Road "The Place of Peace" is equipped with bright floral curtains and upholstered chairs. There are comfortable small wards for those seriously afflicted and homes where the more fortunate families can build a life together. For children actually born in Shanti Nagar there is a crèche where they can be shielded from the disease should this be necessary. Wondrously, such protection is frequently unnecessary for many of the children are able to live with parents whose illness has been arrested and who are well on the way to recovery.

The success of the enterprise can only be measured in terms of the joy that "has made the desert bloom" – for the small town for those whom no-one wanted abounds with love, and something potentially ugly had been made unaccountably beautiful. The secret lies in a combination of Christian compassion and medical competence but above all, in the conviction that the work performed is done for Christ. Speaking to Co-Workers in America in June, 1974, Mother Teresa drew on the example of a Brother who believed he had a special calling to work with lepers.

"A few weeks ago one of our Brothers came in a very terrible distress to me. He had had some difficulty with his Superior, and he kept on saying to me, 'My vocation is to work for lepers. I want to spend myself for the lepers. My vocation is to work for the lepers.' I looked at him and I smiled at him and I said, 'Brother, your vocation is not to work for the lepers, your vocation is to belong to Jesus.' He understood and it changed him completely."

Total dedication to a purely human need, commendable though it be, is not enough. It is the recognition of the vulnerable Christ present in that need, the identification of the Creator with the created and the complete surrender to his service and his will, which confronts the individual with the limitlessness of the mystical and effects what in a less cynical age would undoubtedly be viewed as the miraculous.

# CHAPTER FOUR

## A UNIVERSAL MISSION

# The man who casts off all desires and walks without desire, with no thought of a mine and of an I, comes into peace.

THE BHAGAVAD-GĪTĀ

For ten years after the inception of the Congregation of the Missionaries of Charity, the work amongst those who were most in need of love and care remained within the confines of the diocese of Calcutta. Canon Law forbids the opening of further houses outside the diocese by Institutes less than ten years old and the Archbishop of Calcutta was most emphatic in enforcing this rule. Doubtless this restriction was initially a source of some frustration to Mother Teresa but she has since accepted its wisdom. Ten years in which to shape some of her Sisters into Superiors capable of taking charge of new foundations elsewhere was perhaps not altogether excessive. When, however, in 1960, the ten years of probation prescribed by the Roman Catholic Church were complete, the Sisters were eager to practise the work pattern, begun in Calcutta, throughout India. Almost immediately they were invited to establish houses in Ranchi, Delhi and Jhansi, for news of their work was spreading and bishops in need of their services welcomed them readily into their dioceses. In Delhi the Missionaries of Charity opened a children's home. Its inaugural ceremony was attended by the

Prime Minister, Mr Nehru who, when asked by Mother Teresa if she should tell him about the work of the Congregation, paid the finest possible tribute to ten years of loving service to India's poor: "No, Mother," was his simple reply, "you need not tell me about your work, I know about it. That is why I have come."

The work, which had already won the respect of a man who for many years had given voice to the views of the people of India, spread to many other towns and cities – even to the glamour city of Bombay which prided itself on a display of palatial mansions and an abundance of Catholic schools, colleges and charitable institutions. Mother Teresa wished to open a house in this centre of trade and banking not only because she hoped to find vocations among the well-educated Catholic community in the see of India's first Cardinal, but also because of a conviction that even the pride of India must have its needs. Accordingly she offered her services to Cardinal Gracias, who responded instantly with an invitation to the Missionaries of Charity to come and work in his archdiocese. As Head of the Roman Catholic Church in Bombay, Cardinal Gracias, had already identified many areas of need which his limited number of clergy could not meet. The services of world-wide religious orders of men and congregations of women were therefore particularly welcome and the Missionaries of Charity were given his sincere support.

A short tour of inspection of Bombay was concluded by Mother Teresa's unpopular comment that the slums of Bombay were even worse than the slums of Calcutta. The citizens of Bombay were reluctant to admit that the city which boasted an impressive marine drive and opulent villas also embraced heavily overcrowded "chawls", buildings which rose several storeys high, where ventilation was minimal, the only available water had to be carried up narrow stairways and children had nowhere to play or even breathe fresh air. Yet the uncared for of Bombay were crying out as vociferously for love as the inhabitants of the Calcutta "bustees". Not so very long after the arrival of the Missionaries of Charity in the capital, a newspaper headline depicted the fate of a woman who had died alone and untended in one of the city streets. Her body had remained there for several hours before anyone came to remove it. The

*"We are not social workers but contemplatives in the world."*

69

pattern of need was repeating itself. With the help of the Cardinal, Mother Teresa opened a home for the dying in Bombay.

The unlimited love which the Missionaries of Charity devoted to their Lord must it seemed, be as unlimited in its spheres of application. It grew to embrace all aspects of life: clinics for those suffering from tuberculosis, ante-natal clinics, general dispensaries, mobile leprosy clinics, homes for abandoned children, homes for the dying and the destitute, nursery classes and crèches, primary schools, secondary schools, provision for further education, feeding programmes, villages for leprosy sufferers, commercial schools, training in carpentry, metal work, embroidery, needlework or other skills, child-care and home management, and aid in the event of emergencies and disasters arising from riots, epidemics, famine and flooding – whatever witness to the love of God for men might be required, the Missionaries of Charity and their helpers endeavoured to supply it. In late 1977 a cyclone which hit the state of Andhra Pradesh made two million people homeless and the accompanying floods and devastation took the lives of thousands. A tidal wave, described by an eye-witness as a wall of water eighteen feet high, swept inland for fifteen miles destroying everything in its path. Mother Teresa immediately gathered together a group of Sisters to help the afflicted. Her verdict when confronted by the scenes of desolation was one of horror: "Nowhere have I experienced such utter destruction, such hopeless suffering, such an appalling stench of death". Yet the response was instantaneous and constructive. In the middle of the disaster area she established a house with ten Sisters and, together with Christian Aid, the Red Cross and two other charities they worked round the clock feeding, housing, clothing and inoculating an endless stream of bewildered people, too dazed and too shocked to seek out and reconstruct their own homes. This incident with all its accompanying terror was only one of many which called upon supreme reserves of energy, courage and above all faith, reflected with that distinctive mingling of humility and joy which bears a remarkable witness to the God they serve and which makes the "success" of their labours seem mysteriously unremarkable.

Today the foundations of the Missionary Sisters of

Charity number at least ninety-six in India alone and the commitment of these people, who are themselves of many different nationalities, to Christ in his distressing disguise is by no means restricted to the Indian continent. When Pope Paul VI gave his car to Mother Teresa at the Eucharistic Congress in Bombay in 1964 he did so in order that it should be put towards what he described as her "Universal Mission of love". At that time her mission, although earning an ever-increasing amount of public recognition and acclaim, was still relatively small; today the following list of the foundations outside India projects Pope Paul's comment into the realms of the prophetic:

1  Cocorote, Venezuela    26th July 1965

2  Rome, Italy    22nd August 1968 (Vicolo Tor Fiscale)

3  Tabora, Tanzania    8th September 1968

4  Bourke, Australia    13th September 1969

5  Catia La Mar, Venezuela    19th March 1970

6  Melbourne, Australia    27th April 1970

7  Amman, Jordan    16th July 1970

8  Marin, Venezuela    21st November 1970

9  Southall, London, England    8th December 1970

10  London W.9, England    14th July 1971

11  Bronx, New York, USA    18th October 1971

12  Khulna, Bangladesh    11th February 1972

13  Dacca, Bangladesh    21st February 1972

14  Mauritius    15th August 1972

15  Gaza, Israel    26th February 1973

16  Katherine, Australia    25th March 1973

17  Hodeidah, Yemen Arab Republic    22nd August 1973

18  Lima, Peru    4th October 1973

19  Belfast    1972

20  Addis Ababa, Ethiopia    23rd November 1973

21  Hanubade, Papua, New Guinea    28th May 1974

22  Palermo, Sicily    9th June 1974

23  Tokarara, Papua, New Guinea    18th July 1974

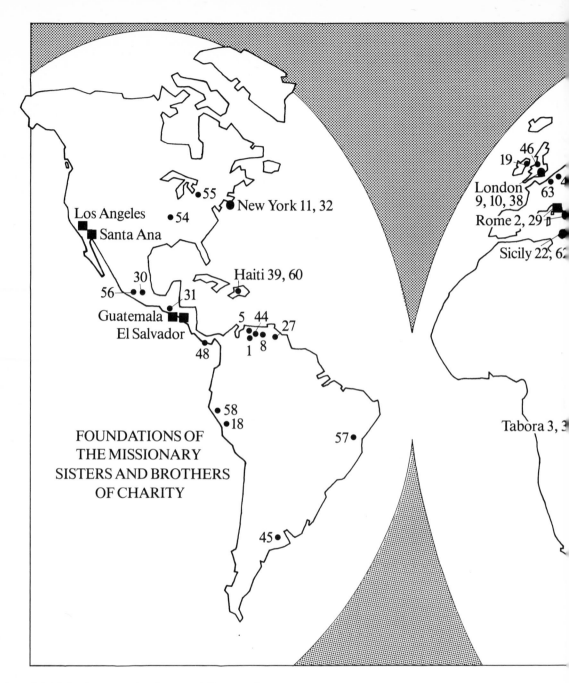

FOUNDATIONS OF
THE MISSIONARY
SISTERS AND BROTHERS
OF CHARITY

New York 11, 32

Los Angeles
Santa Ana
54
55

30
56
31

Haiti 39, 60

Guatemala
El Salvador
5  44
27
1  8
48

58
18

57

45

19  46
London
9, 10, 38  63
Rome 2, 29
Sicily 22, 6

Tabora 3, 3

24  Taiz, Yemen Arab Republic    11th August 1974

25  Mausaid, Bangladesh    25th October 1974

26  Naples, Italy    16th June 1975

27  Ciudad Guayana, Venezuela    4th November 1975

28  Sanor, Yemen Arab Republic    2nd February 1976

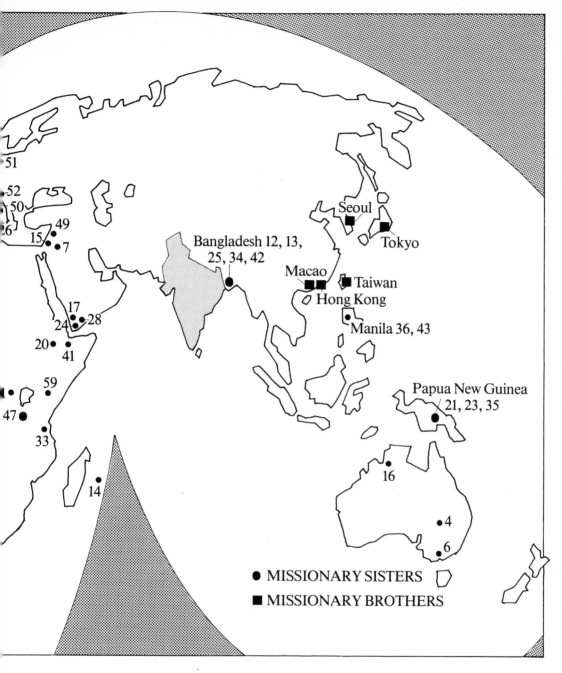

51

52
50
6
15 49
7

Bangladesh 12, 13,
25, 34, 42

Seoul

Tokyo

Macao
Hong Kong
Taiwan

17
24 28
20 41

Manila 36, 43

Papua New Guinea
21, 23, 35

59
47

16

33

4

14

6

● MISSIONARY SISTERS

■ MISSIONARY BROTHERS

29  Rome, Italy    23rd February 1976
      (Pza San Gregorio al Cielo)

30  Mexico City, Mexico    8th April 1976

31  Guatemala City, Guatemala    26th April 1976

32  Bronx, New York (Contemplative)    25th June 1976

42 Syhlet, Bangladesh    1978

°43 Metro-Manila, Philippines    11th February 1978

44 Caracas, Venezuela    30th April 1978

45 Zarate, Argentina    24th May 1978

46 Liverpool, England    21st July 1978

47 Dadoma, Tabora, Tanzania    September 1978

48 El Dorado, Panama    15th September 1978

49 Beirut, Lebanon    10th March 1979

50 Reggio, Calabria, Italy    31st May 1979

51 Essen, West Germany    7th June 1979

52 Zagreb, Yugoslavia    8th June 1979

53 Corato (Bari) Italy    22nd June 1979

54 St Louis, Missouri, USA    22nd June 1979

55 Detroit, Michigan, USA    22nd June 1979

56 Toluca, Mexico    16th July 1979

57 Salvador-Bahia, Brazil    16th July 1979

58 Chimbote, Peru    16th July 1979

59 Nairobi, Kenya    16th July 1979

60 Sanfil, Haiti    August 1979

61 Kigali, Rwanda    29th September 1979

62 Ragusa, Italy    November 1979

63 Ghent, Belgium    13th June 1980

A new foundation is in the process of being established in
Marseille, France.

A report for the Missionary Sisters of Charity for the year 1979 gives some idea of the scope and volume of their work:

| | | | |
|---|---|---|---|
| Foundations | 158 | Slum Schools | 107 |
| Sisters: Professed | 1,187 | Number of | |
| Sisters: Novices | 411 | Children | 15,815 |
| Sisters: Postulants | 120 | Commercial Classes | 10 |
| Dying Assisted | 2,876 | Number of Girls | 441 |
| First Holy | | Sewing Classes | 140 |
| Communion | 6,697 | Number of Girls | 7,335 |
| Confirmation | 2,829 | Sunday Schools | 323 |
| Catechism Centres | 138 | Number of Children | 41,023 |
| Number of members | 6,453 | Feeding Centres | 120 |
| Families Instructed | 3,676 | Number of Persons | 165,338 |
| Marriages Settled | 514 | Malnutrition Centres | 64 |
| Catholic Action Groups | 100 | Number of | |
| Number of Members | 3,500 | Children | 10,988 |
| Mobile Clinics | 495 | Prisons Visited | 15 |
| Number of | | Day Creches | 12 |
| Patients | 4,105,604 | Number of Children | 898 |
| Leprosy Centres | 103 | Hospitals Visited | 84 |
| Number of | | Night Shelters | 5 |
| Patients | 258,445 | Number of Persons | 774 |
| Leprosy | | Christmas Treat: | |
| Rehabilitation Centres | 8 | Children | 44,207 |
| Number of Patients | 1,942 | Families | 14,516 |
| Home for Dying and | | Families Consecrated | |
| Sick Destitutes | 63 | to the Sacred Heart | 981 |
| Admissions | 7,632 | Mother and Child | |
| Home for Abandoned | | Care Centres | 6 |
| Children | 49 | Number of Persons | 4,018 |
| Admissions | 2,770 | Food and Clothing | |
| Families Visited | 82,233 | Distribution | 50,962 |
| Natural Family | | Homes for Alcoholics | |
| Planning Centres | 161 | and Drug Addicts | 7 |
| Number of Cases | 194,344 | Admissions | 505 |

The dramatic contrast between the recollection of a single woman leaving behind her the security of the Loreto Convent and stepping out to live amongst the poorest of the poor in the slums of Calcutta and a mission which is now indeed universal invites a multitude of questions, not least of them the simple interrogative "how?" Yet the contrast be-

*A moment of mourning among the Missionaries of Charity and the Co-Workers for those who have died in their care.*

tween the "then" and the "now" is not as great as it might at first seem to a world which has come to regard complex structures, vast organisations and a plethora of bureaucrats as essential components of any activity which takes place at an international level. The spirit of the Society and its work have remained unchanged by such considerations as the number of people with whom it deals or the geographical location of the foundations, perhaps because Mother Teresa insists that her mission is with the individual and not the collective. "Our daily contact is with men who do not even have a piece of bread to eat. Our mission is to look at the problem more individually – and not collectively. We care for a person, and not for a multitude. We seek the person

with whom Jesus identified himself, when he said: 'I was hungry. I was sick.' If we looked at the question in a generic way, we would almost not have the courage to do anything." Individuals, she insists, are the same in every country. They have the same essential physical and spiritual needs. Mother Teresa's work has spread from Calcutta all over India, and to many other parts of the world, but in every case she and her helpers feed the hungry, clothe the naked, nurse the sick and dying and give comfort to the afflicted, and in every case their service is an attempt to confirm the words of St Matthew's gospel (25:35), "For I was hungry and you gave me food, I was thirsty and you gave me drink, I was a stranger and you welcomed me, I was naked and you clothed me, I was sick and you visited me, I was in prison and you came to me".

"Our discernment of aid is only ever the necessity": Mother Teresa's statement so simply expressed conceals a wealth of complexity demanding unlimited resources of courage and compassion, for "necessity" has manifested itself in a multitude of ways. When in 1965 the Missionaries of Charity were invited by a bishop to go to Venezuela it was to help meet the spiritual needs of the millions of baptised Roman Catholics in Latin America who had lapsed in their faith largely because of the lack of priests and religious to instruct and guide them. The Sisters were given the right to conduct funeral services, they took Holy Communion to the sick, washed and cleansed the elderly, fed and clothed the hungry and the poor and when in 1972 strong winds swept the coast of Venezuela leaving many homes without a roof, they inevitably became volunteer roof repairers.

In 1968 came the invitation to work amongst the poor of Rome. The request was made by the Holy Father himself and to Mother Teresa's strong ecclesiastical sense the opportunity to serve at the very centre of Christianity was not to be declined. The Sisters moved into a slum area and worked with the refugees from Sicily and Sardinia who could only obtain unskilled work and who were not entitled to such State benefits as medical schemes and social security.

In Australia, the call came from Archbishop Knox for the Missionaries of Charity to come to Melbourne. "Necessity" this time took the form, not of extreme physical poverty, starvation or of destitutes dying in the streets but

rather of drug addicts, alcoholics, prisoners in need of rehabilitation and juvenile delinquents crying out for
attention.

When in 1970, Mother Teresa visited England she was
taken on a tour of the night spots of London by the Simon
Community, a charity which cares for the derelicts, the
alcoholics, the drug addicts and the "down-and-outs" of the
metropolis. She saw the strip clubs of Soho, she was shown
the people sleeping under the tarpaulins which draped the
scaffolding of St Martin-in-the-Fields and she found the
tramps curled up on the gratings where warm air rises from
the kitchens of the London hotels. Among the methylated

*Cardinal Hume pays a surprise visit to the London tramps' party.*

spirit drinkers and the drug pushers a young man, well-fed
and well-dressed, took an overdose of barbiturates before
her very eyes. The "necessity" of the affluent Western world
was for the kind of love which could combat its mental,
emotional and spiritual poverty. The poorest of the poor
need not necessarily be those suffering from physical
deprivation. The recognition of this crucial fact brought the
Missionaries of Charity to London to found Homes of

Compassion for destitute men and women, to feed the "down-and-outs" on the banks of a city canal and to knock on the doors of the lonely and the elderly.

In the East End of London one row of council houses in particular cried out desperately for attention. They were and still are occupied for the most part by patients who have been discharged from mental hospitals but who are frequently still unable to look after themselves. Sister Marie-Celine, the Indian Sister Superior in London, has vivid memories of one of these houses occupied by an elderly woman who refused to open the door to anyone: "The Sisters came knocking every day because they had noticed a nasty smell when they were going past. In the end one of them put her foot in the door and the woman had to let her in. There were two rooms. In one of them the toilet was blocked and in both rooms everything was covered with its contents. The Sisters borrowed shovels and filled five sacks with faeces. They washed and they cleaned the curtains, furniture – everything, and while they were doing it the woman came to one of them and said: 'Do you still love me now?' Do you know what the Sister answered?" Sister Marie-Celine's delight was obvious. "She said, 'I love you even more now.'" The episode, appalling as it was, was by no means an isolated incident and nor was need of this kind confined to London.

The apparent wealth of other European cities and of the USA concealed a similar form of poverty. In 1971 the Missionaries of Charity set up their convent in the very heart of the South Bronx area of New York where even the local police do not dare to venture alone. Outside their simple building the Sisters have created a small haven of green where they keep chickens undeterred by the fact that the outside walls of their chapel, the interior of which is dominated by the words "I thirst", are sometimes daubed in two-foot high letters with such slogans as "Sons of Satan". Mother Teresa's reaction is one of unmitigated joy: "The Sisters are doing small things in New York, helping the children, visiting the lonely, the sick, the unwanted. We know now that being unwanted is the greatest disease of all. That is the poverty we find around us here. In one of the houses where the Sisters visit, a woman living alone was dead many days before she was found, and she was found because her body had begun to decompose. The people around her did not know her name. When someone told me that the Sisters had not started any big work, that they are doing small things quietly, I said that even if they helped one person, that was alright. Jesus would have died for one person, for one sinner."

Christian love must take little account of personal risk and Mother Teresa's "discernment of aid" is uninfluenced by concern for the danger involved. Where there is strife or discord or disaster there is a special need for that spirit of love and forgiveness which for the Christian finds its ultimate expression in the crucifixion. In the first few months of its life as a new nation, tragedy struck Bangladesh, formerly East Pakistan. In October 1970 a cyclone drowned more than 300,000 people in one of the worst natural disasters of the 20th century and in the following year occupation by West Pakistan troops claimed a further three million lives. 200,000 women were reported to have been raped and while nearly 10,000,000 men, women and children fled to India to escape the violence, Mother Teresa and two teams of Missionaries of Charity rushed to do what they could in the stricken country. The victims of rape were to suffer particularly from rejection by their own families. Muslim tradition dictated that despite the fact that they had been violated against their will, these girls would be abandoned. Some of the Freedom Fighters who had fought for the liberation of East Pakistan made a dramatic break with Muslim custom by offering to marry these "heroines of the nation" and the Prime Minister, Sheikh Mujibar Rahman, called upon the Bangladeshi to recognise the sacrifices of their women and to honour them rather than punish them, but there were still many who were reduced to committing suicide by tying their saris round their throats.

Mother Teresa set up a home in Dacca and several more in Bangladesh to care for these women and girls. Fewer of the violated women came forward than had been anticipated and so the Sisters explored the needs of the surrounding villages. They opened clinics and gave practical training to women who were not equipped to fend for themselves without their men. In one village in particular, out of twenty-three male heads of families, seventeen had been shot in one day. The village had then been put to the torch and most of the homes were destroyed. The widows, unprepared for work which would raise money for their families, were begging on

*"If the Sisters help only one person, that is alright. Jesus would have died for one person, for one sinner."*

80

the streets of Dacca. The reaction of one of the Sisters was unhesitatingly practical: "Every Bengali woman knows how to make puffed rice. With a little help we can start a business here in this 'widows' village'." Immediately she began to plan and work with the women, their puffed rice was sold in the Dacca market and their fatherless children did not go hungry.

In 1971 Mother Teresa took four Sisters to Belfast, to a place where hatred was preached even from the church pulpits. A report in a newsletter for that year, describes their arrival:

*"The four Sisters, equipped with two blankets each and a violin, were to take up residence in the Catholic 'ghetto' of Ballymurphy – in a Council house, which had previously been occupied by Father Hugh Mullan, a curate of the parish. The house was now empty because Father Mullan had been shot dead by 'the forces of law and order' as he had just finished administering Extreme Unction to a wounded man. This is the kind of mad situation in which the Sisters now find themselves, into which they will try to bring some spark of love, forgiveness and understanding; 'where there is hatred may we bring love, where there is wrong, may we bring the spirit of forgiveness'.*
*The house was completely empty, bereft of all furniture. It had also been ransacked by vandals while it was standing tenantless. Mother Teresa said that the two neighbouring houses had also been rented by the parish. She plans to have a small group of Anglican nuns working with her own Sisters there – a sign of unity in a strife-torn city."*

In the midst of tragedy and bitterness the Sisters set about quietly helping the local people and their children. The door of their home was always open as a refuge from violence and desolation, yet a visitor to the house some time after their arrival in Belfast describes how during a prolonged shooting match between Springhill (Catholics) and Springwater (an adjoining Protestant area), the Sisters were reduced to sitting on the stairs for four hours because it was the only relatively safe place for those who had shown so little regard for their own safety.

In Peru the Missionaries of Charity established a home for abandoned children, paralysed young adults and old men and women in a large dirty pink convent at the heart of the "thieves' market", in one of the poorest districts of Lima. During the disturbances between the enemy and the police which were witnessed by many an overseas television screen in February 1975, the home shook with the rumblings of tanks passing the door, and bullet holes in the dispensary and chapel windows show how exposed the occupants were to the hazards of life in Lima.

*"In Africa also there are God's poor and the Sisters are there with them."*

In Gaza the Sisters offered love and care to the deprived Arabic speaking people living in Israeli-occupied territory. During the uncertainty of the cease-fire they searched amongst the 380,000 Arab refugees who had been squeezed into Gaza by the tide of armies fighting in 1948, 1956 and 1967, for the poorest of the poor. In Gaza Old Town they took over a house once occupied by a priest who, cut off by the barriers of war and politics, had undertaken a lonely struggle to keep the faith. The priest had been killed shortly before their arrival, in a murder which reflected the violence and tension of the area. In a matter of weeks, however, the Missionaries of Charity cleaned the house and the neighbouring church and banished the fear and the sorrow of many whose lives had appeared without hope.

Mother Teresa's instruction to those who work with her in such circumstances is the simple directive: "Begin in a small way. Don't look for numbers. Every small act of love for the unwanted and the poor is important to Jesus." Achievements which have won the recognition and admiration of the world are dismissed with the unquestionably sincere explanation: "All of us are but his instruments, who do our little bit and pass by." The string of interrogatives which present themselves when confronted by the disparity between the smallness of the apparent intention, the humility of the "instruments" – and the magnitude of the end result are gently quashed with a reminder of Christ's own words: "Jesus has said that we are much more important to his Father, than the grass, and the birds, and the flowers of the Earth." "Every human being", she insists, "comes from the hand of God and we all know what is the love of God for us". The answer lies in the placing of the self at the complete disposal of the God whose love for his creation is indisputable and to whom all things are possible. It lies in a faith which involves the abandoning of self-will in order to allow the operation of a will which is much greater, much wiser and manifestly more effective.

The spirit of poverty, so fundamental to the Order of the Missionaries of Charity, is in itself not only a means of identification with those whom they serve but also an expression of faith in Divine Providence. For this reason Mother Teresa has stressed repeatedly that fund-raising for her work is contrary to her wishes and declined all offers of a regular income for the Sisters: "I don't want the work to become a business but to remain a work of love. I want you to have that complete confidence that God won't let us down. Take him at his word and seek first the kingdom of heaven, and all else will be added on. Joy, peace and unity are more important than money. If God wants me to do something, he gives me the money. I refused an offer from Cardinal Cook of five hundred dollars a month for each Sister working in Harlem. I said to him: 'Do you think, Your Eminence, that God is going to become bankrupt in New York?'" Her response to suggestions that finance must be considered might be seen by some as infuriatingly impractical: "Money – I don't think about it. It always comes. The Lord sends it. We do his work. He provides the

*"All of us are but his instruments who do our little bit and pass by."*

85

means. If he does not give us the means that shows that he does not want the work so why worry?"

To many complete confidence in the love and benevolence of God does not come quite so readily; to some it appears as irresponsible, to others as enviable but restricted to the limited number of saints and prophets who pass through this world. Yet Mother Teresa's conviction that everything will be well is by no means unique or élitist. She is echoing not only the words of her Lord but also the belief of every authentic Buddhist mystic, who will claim an inner security based on the conviction that everything is alright even in the very midst of suffering, and of countless Christian writers, among them most notably Julian of Norwich who in her "Revelations of Divine Love" recorded those much-quoted words, "All thing shall be well". Nor was the revelation to Julian of Norwich confined to this statement for in it her Lord went on to say, "Thou shalt see thyself that all manner of thing shall be well". Not only, it seems, was everything subject to a divine order which would guarantee its goodness but, by the grace of God, that order would not remain totally incomprehensible but would be made recognisable and apparent. To Mother Teresa there can be no question of Divine Providence remaining unrecognisable: "Christ has proved what he said – that we are more important to his Father than the flowers of the field, than the birds of the air and so on. It really is true. We have no income whatsoever, and yet things are just pouring in." ... "There has not been one single day that we have refused somebody, that we did not have food, that we did not have a bed or something, and we deal with thousands of people. We have 53,000 lepers and yet never one has been sent away because we did not have. It is always there although we have no salaries. We receive freely and give freely. This has been such a beautiful gift of God."

In a scientific age she believes there is still room for the miraculous: "In Calcutta there were floods and we worked day and night cooking for 5,000 people. The army gave us food. One day, something told me to turn off the road toward an unknown area, and we found a little village where people were being swept away. We got boats for them. We found out later that if we had come only two hours later they would have all been drowned. Then I said to the bishop that I

*Above left: "Being unwanted is the worst disease that any human being can experience."*
*Left: "Joy is a net of love by which you can catch souls."*

was going to ask our novices to pray for the rain, which had been pouring down for many days, to stop. I told him, 'The novices are very earnest. They pray with great energy. It will be a strong expression.' So we put them – 178 of them – in the church of our mission. Outside it was raining; inside they began to pray, and I brought out the Blessed Sacrament. After a while I went to the door of the church and looked out. The rain had stopped and there was a patch of clear sky above us – yes, I believe in miracles."

*"The poverty of the West is far more difficult to solve than the poverty of India."*

One such incident is easily dismissed as coincidence, but as the pattern of needs supplied accumulates there comes a point where "coincidence" ceases to be an adequate explanation. Speaking in the Carmelite Church in Dublin in 1979, Mother Teresa recalled another occasion where the needs of the hungry were "mysteriously" met: "In Calcutta alone we cook for 7,000 people every day and if one day we do not cook they do not eat. And this one Friday morning

Sister came and told me: 'Mother, Friday-Saturday, there is no food, we will have to tell the people we have nothing to give today and tomorrow.' I had no words, I had nothing to say to her but by nine o'clock the Government for some reason, unknown reason, closed all the schools and all the bread that would have been given to the children was sent to us and our children and our 7,000 people ate bread for two days. They had never eaten so much bread in their lives! Nobody in the whole city knew why the schools were closed

*Among the homeless and the lonely of Liverpool – an interlude of joy.*

but I knew. I knew the delicate thoughtfulness of God, such a delicate love."

On one occasion, a Sister telephoned from Agra to say that they were desperately in need of a children's home which would cost 50,000 rupees. Mother Teresa did not have the money: "I told her it was impossible. Then the telephone rang again. This time it was from a newspaper, saying I'd been given the Magsaysay Award from the Philippines. I asked, 'How much is it?' The man replied, 'About fifty thousand rupees, Mother'. So I called the Sister back to tell her God must want a children's home in Agra."

In 1971 Mother Teresa visited England. She had been planning to start a novitiate outside India and by the time she arrived in England the choice of possible locations had been narrowed down to Dublin or London. One of her first visits in England was to a priest in Southall who wished to consult her about problems among the immigrant community. In the course of her visit it was suggested that Mother Teresa brought her novitiate to Southall and it was agreed that if within two weeks she had heard nothing from the Bishop of Dublin, she would do so. A fortnight passed by and nothing was heard so Mother Teresa sought amongst the properties of Southall for a suitable house. The ideal place was found but the asking price was £9,000. Mother Teresa insisted that she could not pay more than £6,000 but, as always when she has found a possible house for her Sisters, she tossed a religious medal into the garden of the property. By the time Mother Teresa had returned to the priest in Southall, the estate agent had telephoned to say that the owner was prepared to sell for £6,000 because she wanted the house to be filled with love. Mother Teresa still did not have the necessary funds in England and money could not be taken out of India. As planned, however, she set off on a tour around England during which she mentioned the possibility of opening a novitiate in Southall. She made no appeal whatsoever for money but by the end of her tour the old knitting bag which she carries with her, had been stuffed full of donations. The total, when the gifts were counted, amounted to £5,995. The house in Southall was obviously meant to be.

Experiences of this kind are almost innumerable and by no means confined to Mother Teresa herself. "When I first went from Bombay to Calcutta to find Mother Teresa", one Sister confided, "I wanted to join the Order but Mother said that perhaps I should sort my health out first. The doctors were telling me I must have the operation but I felt that if I went back to Bombay for surgery I might never return so I decided to stay. Mother gave me one of her medals and I prayed. I never had the operation and for some reason I have never needed it." A Co-Worker remembers one Christmas when for some reason the usual flood of provisions had not flowed into the London home for the tramps' Christmas party which is held there annually. Reluctant to use money which had been allocated for other needs, but determined that the tramps should have their Christmas, she went home and prayed. On the following morning the first letter she opened contained a cheque for £1,000 from someone who, having witnessed one of these Christmas parties, specifically requested that the money be put towards the celebrations for the city's "down-and-outs".

*In Hong Kong, a small boy learns at an early age the tragedy of being alone and unwanted.*

Another Co-Worker recalls an occasion on which she had been invited to speak. Several other speakers preceded her and as her turn drew nearer she realised that everything that she had intended to say in her prepared speech had already been said. In the short interval which preceded her own talk she went, feeling somewhat apprehensive, to the chapel and in the figure of Christ crucified she found the subject matter for a talk which she delivered without further preparation. The response to it was warm. Those who knew the person concerned remarked upon a "difference". From that day on, like Mother Teresa, she never prepared her talks other than with a prayer.

Any one of these incidents, considered in isolation, could be readily attributed to chance or coincidence but for many who experience such occurrences there comes a point where they are made somehow aware that their own familiar lives interact with the lives of others to form a pattern, for which coincidence appears an inadequate explanation and in which there is an inescapable sense of higher purpose. To the Missionaries of Charity the recognition of this "higher purpose" is something so fundamental and so totally accepted in their lives that at times it becomes a source of amusement. An

endearing story tells how, during a hard winter in New York, a car ground to a halt outside the Sisters' house. Eager to help, they rushed out and managed to push the vehicle out of the snowdrift. Only a short time later a second car came to grief in the same spot and the Sisters were once again ready to rush to the driver's assistance. By this time, however, it was late and the Sister in charge directed the others to go to their beds while she went to the chapel to pray. On her knees she asked for help and within minutes she heard the sound of a snow plough arriving. Once more she sank to her knees, this time to thank the Almighty for answering her prayer, but minutes later another snow plough arrived. In desperation, she prayed again: "Lord, that's enough. No more snow ploughs please!" The story is recounted now with much hilarity.

*Christmas cards designed by Co-Workers brought support for those whose work was a continued witness to faith in Divine Providence.*

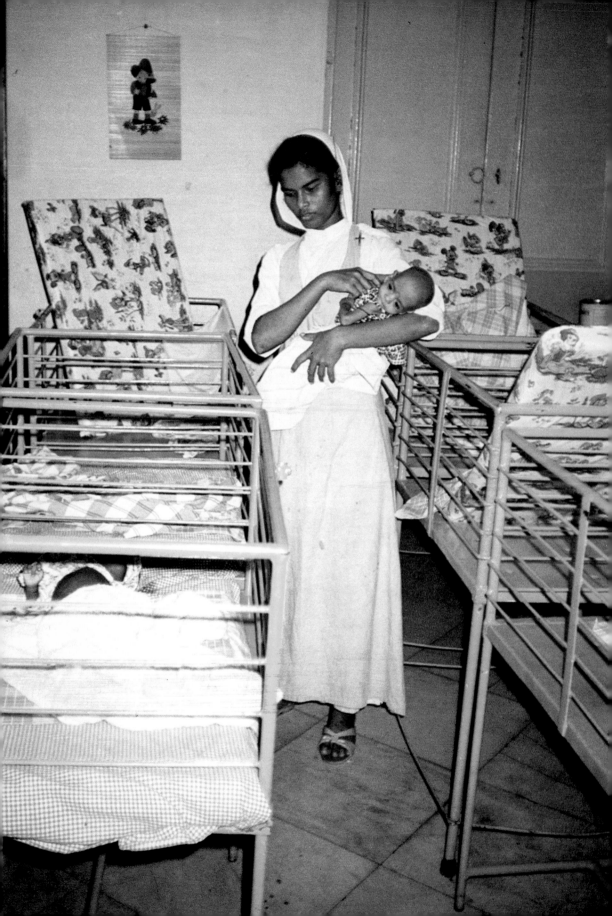

In the early days of the Order such unprotesting faith, such conviction that the hand of God is everywhere apparent might not have come so readily and so easily and even now there must be times when the presence of a benevolent Lord is not so obvious. A letter from Tabora, Tanzania, gives a very vivid insight into some of the difficulties which confront the Missionaries of Charity:

*"I experienced one of the worst days of my life on the 14th March. Early in the morning, one of the old men in our home came and called me, saying that another of the old men had died. I thought it was the usual heart failure, but when I went in I had the greatest shock of my life – the wall in one of our rooms had fallen in on the old man and he was stone dead. We had been having heavy rain, but we did not realise that there was dampness in the foundations, as a matter of fact one cannot see the dampness at all. The police were very good and helpful.*

*"Then one of our ladies, while yawning, dislocated her jaw, so I had to drive her to hospital in the pouring rain. Our car, which is a huge affair and as old as can be, is not suited for this country at all as the clearance is very low, so each time I go down a road the bottom of the car hits the corrugations on the roads which are made of red sand only. The car, being very heavy, often gets stuck, as the only type of car that can run here is one with a four-wheel drive.*

*In Calcutta, Co-Workers of different nationalities and faiths are united in a common concern for the city's unwanted children.*

95

*"When I came home we started re-arranging the house in order to fit in everyone, and it was nearly night before everything was settled. When one of our ladies cried out for help I thought another wall had fallen, but when I rushed to the scene, I saw a poisonous snake gliding round the room. Thank God, one of our workers saw it and rushed in with a stick and killed it. So ended the day!*

*"We are due for a lot more rain they say, so I ask for your prayers that our house stands, as it is very old, and that our car, which is also very old, does not get stuck in the mud."*

*From the Bronx, New York, another Sister writes during a "Leisure Programme" for the Inner City Kids: "The work is exhausting, and we long for Thursday, the one free day. From early morning till late in the evening, often into the night we are on our feet and alert, for the whole house is full of children from six to sixteen filling all the rooms, streaming*

*An ambulance provided by the Co-Workers of Weybridge brings treatment to those areas where it is most needed.*

*through doors, house, courtyard, garden; climbing walls, hanging from trees, scattering playthings, making everything dirty, eating half their sandwiches and throwing the other half into the dustbin, drinking their orange juice and firing the unopened cellophane packets into the pools. Every Wednesday a bus arrives with various things. New York and other cities spend an enormous amount of money for thousands of Ghetto children. Mobile swimming pools, films, puppet shows on the streets, free tickets to the zoo and museums, as well as the daily lunch, with a carton of milk and fruit juice, and sandwiches. This is the difficulty, everything for the body, nothing much for the mind and soul. For the mind* must *be active, it cannot stay passive – it shrivels up, it becomes stunted. The body gets an unbearable abundance and one is thrown off a normal course. Each summer sees more and more criminal activity, and that is caused not only by the heat."*

Despite difficulties, dangers and personal hardships, however, Mother Teresa and many with her have been able to recognise in every act of human love, be it the self-denial of a small child or the gift of ICI's Laboratory Building in its own compound of five acres, the "proof" of an eternal love. Thomas Kelly, the Quaker, once wrote of this very recognition: "There is an experience of the Eternal breaking into time, which transforms all life into a miracle of faith and action. Unspeakable, profound and full of glory as an inward experience, it is the root of concern for all creation, the true ground of social endeavour."

The "transformation" to which he refers and the fact that the simple but reassuring prediction "Thou shalt see thyself that all manner of thing shall be well" has been repeatedly realised means that the guidance of a Divine Providence can be identified in the very midst of adversity and chaos.

*"A month ago", writes a Sister in Dacca, "we were taken to a place which is really a group of small islands. These isles suffer yearly from a cyclone. On Chor Alexander and Chor Falcon (Chor is the word for isle), we had a lot of work among the destitutes. We met a woman who was thrown into the River Meghna during the cyclone and in her struggle for safety she got hold of a python. And the good python pulled her to another Chor and left her on dry land without any harm. Three days after a fisherman rescued her. Similarly, even crocodiles also, saved a few people. How wonderful are the ways of God!"*

Mother Teresa was able to see even the fighting and the flooding in Bangladesh as a "blessing in disguise" for she felt that it had brought out the best in the Indian people. Many had gone without in order to assist the refugees. Even the children had brought an onion or a spoonful of rice and the 4,000 who were being fed daily at Shishu Bhavan and who ate only when the Sisters could provide for them, offered to go without food for a day in order that the refugees might eat. God's presence is manifested at the very heart of catastrophe and so the whole of life including its greatest horrors becomes part of a "miracle of faith".

Caught in the violence and terror of the nine-day civil war, one of the Sisters in Amman, Jordan, kept a diary. The entries record "bombs falling very near – big cannon balls flying like flies, and bullets too". They include an account of how armed men came at night to the house where the Missionaries of Charity were staying and insisted on entering, and of days and nights spent only in the corridor because the glass in the outer rooms had been shattered by heavy artillery.

*"One night while we were praying", writes the Sister, "we suddenly saw a light coming through the door – it was pitch dark and there were no lights, and we never used to burn candles unless it was very necessary, so seeing the light creeping into the room in complete darkness, you can imagine our fear. This light was from search helicopters looking for the enemy."*

Yet there is no suggestion of complaint, no intimation that the Sisters should be anywhere but there, ready to help the afflicted, and when after nine days the fighting ceases, the fact is recorded with a brief comment which is striking only as a witness to a profound faith:

*"Peace was declared, and God was once again our watchful Father, for just as the battle was about to begin in our area, the civil, war stopped".*

The history of the Missionaries of Charity has not been without its apparent "failures". After a relatively short time in Belfast, the Indian Sisters found that they were not wanted and so abandoned the challenge which had appeared to offer itself to them. To Mother Teresa, however, even this retreat proved to be only one more example of a wisdom which passes human understanding. Triumphant even in "failure", to her Co-Workers in Ireland in November 1973 she wrote the following words of reassurance: "Leaving Belfast was a very big sacrifice – but very fruitful – for our Sisters are now going to Ethiopia to feed the hungry Christ. The same Sisters who so lovingly served him in Belfast will now be giving his love and compassion to the suffering people of Ethiopia – pray for them and share with them the joy of loving and serving." In the light of the rather special circumstances which led to the foundation of a house in Addis Ababa, the closing of the Belfast house became part of the miraculous intervention of Divine Providence.

Mother Teresa, en route from Rome to Hodeidah, shortly after the Sisters had left Belfast, broke her journey in Addis Ababa, in order to investigate the possibilities of reaching out to the poor who were suffering terribly as a result of a drought in Northern Ethiopia. The general opinion of others involved in relief work there, was that it would be impossible to obtain permission for the Sisters to enter the country, but with great difficulty a meeting with the Emperor's daughter was arranged. The Princess showed great interest in the Missionaries of Charity's work of love and compassion among the poorest of the poor, and Mother Teresa was able to ask her to tell her father, Emperor Haile Selassie, that on the occasion of the 43rd anniversary of his coronation which was to be celebrated that week, she would like to offer him the Sisters to help his suffering people. On the following morning Mother Teresa received the news that, despite a day of heavy engagements with Archbishop Makarios, the Emperor would see her that afternoon. A series of questions from the Minister of the Imperial Court preceded the interview:

*"What do you want from the Government?"*
*"Nothing", replied Mother Teresa, "I have only come to offer my Sisters to work among the poor suffering people".*

*"What will your Sisters do?"*
*"We give whole-hearted free service to the poorest of the poor."*

*"What qualifications do they have?"*
*"We try to bring tender love and compassion to the unwanted and the unloved."*

*"I see you have quite a different approach. Do you preach to the people, trying to convert them?"*
*"Our works of love reveal to the suffering poor the love of God for them."*

Mother Teresa was then ushered into the presence of the eighty-year-old Emperor. The encounter was short, the outcome completely contrary to all anticipation and yet somehow inevitable:

"I have heard about the good work you do. I am very happy you have come. Yes, let your Sisters come to Ethiopia."

God had once more performed a miracle of love for his poor.

The Sister left behind in Addis Ababa to find a suitable house, described her search as "a wonderful experience of trust in Divine Providence":

*"I would go out every morning, fervently clinging to my Rosary, meeting Jesus at every corner in the numberless beggars, lepers, the squalid young unwed mother with her baby tied to her back, trusting firmly that I would be guided to the right place. I came across two houses that had the sign 'To Let' up on the window and was very near concluding the contract for one of the houses at a rent of 250 Ethiopian Dollars a month, when I decided to wait another day. Next morning I went out on my usual tour, taking a different direction; I spotted another house with the notice 'To let'."*

It goes almost without saying that the Managing Director of the firm adjoining the house, who initially asked for a rent of 450 Ethiopian Dollars, eventually gave the Missionaries of Charity the use of the property, free of charge.

*"The next step",* the Sister continues, *"was to get the workers to clean up the place as it was in a rather shabby and dirty state, so from Tuesday to Friday I took over the job of supervisor of carpentry, plumbing and white-washing — thank God the head man knew Italian so we somehow managed to make ourselves understood. As for furniture, the parish priest very kindly appealed for some discarded pieces and again — miracle of Providence — three good tables, a cupboard, a gas-cooker, a bench arrived: as for beds, I had managed to get four from the famous Addis Ababa market so when the Sisters arrived on Friday evening we were able to settle down together in our little home."*

From the disappointment of Belfast, something vital and constructive had sprung.

**MISSIONARIES**

**OF CHARITY**

"As long as you did it to one of these My least brethren. You did it to Me"

Send the same letter to U.S. & Germany

My dear Co-Workers,

    God's blessing be with you and your families during 1973 During this year we will all try in a special way to work for Peace. Before we obtain this peace- we must learn from Jesus- to be Meek and humble of Heart. Only Humility will lead us to Unity and Unity to Peace - therefore let us help each other to come so close to Jesus that the lesson of humility we may learn with joy.

       God bless you

       M. Teresa m.c.

Registered Charity C No. 37184 C.T. 8E/14/54-55

In March 1980 a terrible fire swept the three-storey Victorian hostel for homeless women, run by the Missionaries of Charity in Kilburn, London. Nine women were killed, among them, a young Co-Worker who had only been helping there for one day prior to the accident. Another woman was critically injured. The disastrous incident which reached the headlines of the national press and which was attributed by some to overcrowding and the lack of proper fire precautions, was a source of overwhelming grief and shock to the Sisters. Yet Cardinal Hume, who visited the scene at the time, was able to comment that, despite the sadness and difficulty of the circumstances, the Missionaries of Charity were "bearing up well". Asked some time later how she reconciled such a devastating occurrence with a joyous belief in a benevolent God, the Sister Superior was able to explain: "We knew the women so intimately. They were such a united family and they went without much suffering. I knew there was no hope for them in this life. They had no future here really and I am sure they are happy now in a much better place." Much had come of their sacrifice. A relative of the young Co-Worker had been able to say that on the day of her death, he had become a Christian – "It was that or go mad," and Mother Teresa had been able to give thanks for the fact that public and government attention had been inescapably drawn to the conditions under which these people were having to live. "Mother said that it had to happen to us because we have become a symbol of the poor but there are many other hostels in London in need of attention. Now legislation is being passed and support is being given to them."

The recognition of the workings of a God of love at the very centre of disaster requires a special kind of faith, a faith doubtless reinforced by repeated experiences of the way in which something positive may spring from what in purely human terms amounts to the disappointing, the painful and even the tragic, but a faith which is, above all, inextricably linked with the kind of open heart which allows the operation of a Divine Will and so permits it to become recognisable. To Mother Teresa, an open heart of this kind is achieved through prayer:

"Love to pray – feel often during the day the need for prayer and take the trouble to pray. Prayer enlarges the heart until it is capable of containing God's gift of himself. Ask and seek, and your heart will grow big enough to receive him and keep him as your own..."

To the Missionaries of Charity prayer is not set apart from action, as an activity confined to the seclusion of the chapel. Their work as a direct expression of their love for Christ is in itself a prayer, and so Mother Teresa is able to ask of her Co-Workers "Let us learn to pray the work by doing it in his presence: by doing it with him, for him and to him all the twenty-four hours."

Nor is prayer the desperate voicing of a personal, self-centred will:

"Our progress in holiness depends on God and ourselves — on God's grace and on our will to be holy. We must have a real living determination to reach holiness. 'I will be a saint' means I will despoil myself of all that is not God; I will strip my heart of all created things; I will live in poverty and detachment; I will renounce my will, my inclination, my whims and fancies and make myself a willing slave to the will of God..."

It involves submission to a direction which is not always immediately comprehensible or easily acceptable:

"Make sure that you let God's grace work in your souls by accepting whatever he gives you, and giving him whatever he takes from you. True holiness consists in doing God's will with a smile..."

The smile becomes a joyous expression of confidence that in the very darkest hour of the crucifixion, the presence of God is manifest in a spirit of loving forgiveness, "Father, forgive them for they know not what they do", and that agony is followed by a triumphant resurrection born of love. As the sense of being loved grows and deepens, so it becomes an unshakeable source of strength. Armed with this strength, Mother Teresa has been able to follow with utter conviction the example of the Christ who at the very threshold of death was able to say, "Thy will be done". In her often repeated words: "Not I, but Christ who lives in me", lies the key to Thomas Kelly's "profound inward experience which is the root of concern for all creation", and the secret of a peace which, while passing all understanding, dispels all human anxieties.

One of the fundamental teachings of the Bhagavad Gītā,

"The Song of God", is summed up in the words of Krishna, the incarnation of God, to Prince Arjuna:

"The world is imprisoned by its own activity, except where actions are performed as worship of God. Therefore you must perform every action sacramentally, and be free of all attachment to results...

"Mentally resign all your action to me. Regard me as your dearest loved one. Know me as your only refuge. Be united always in heart and consciousness with me. United with me, by my grace, you shall overcome all difficulties."

The growth of what Pope Paul foresaw as a "universal mission of love" has been shaped and directed by a conviction not so very far removed from these words from the Bhagavad Gīta; its future finds its most effective guarantee in St Francis de Sales' gentle promise of a sublime peace:

"Do not look forward to what might happen tomorrow; the same Everlasting Father who cares for you today, will take care of you tomorrow and every day. Either he will shield you from suffering or he will give you unfailing strength to bear it. Be at peace, then, and put aside all anxious thoughts and imaginings."

# CHAPTER FIVE

# THE MISSIONARY BROTHERS OF CHARITY

*"Together we are privileged to be the representatives of love in the lives of the suffering people – representatives of the love of men for their fellow men and of God's special love for the poor and the suffering."*

BROTHER ANDREW, M C

"**P**ray and good things happen! Bad turns into good." With these words, a Japanese priest who had worked with the Missionary Brothers in Tokyo gave expression to his experience of a life in which the presence and love of God could be ever and everywhere invoked. The confident statement struck a very special chord of recognition in Brother Andrew, General Servant of the Missionary Brothers of Charity for like Mother Teresa he looks upon the development of the universal mission and the growth of the Order of Brothers as part of that mission, as an answer to prayer and a miracle of Divine Providence working through all too humble instruments:

*"It is all so fragile, fearfully fragile. We are weak, unqualified, unorganised, unfaithful. And yet there is this very powerful feeling of the presence that can be felt and seen as alive and active and life-giving in so many ways. The ridiculous contrast of our weakness and ineptitude together with a spiritual strength that touches so many lives – rich and poor, young and old, educated and illiterate, Indian and non-Indian, whole and broken. Our leprosy work grows in many ways. We have homes for dying and handicapped people; there are more homeless children with us, more child-feeding programmes and little slum schools, etc. And the miracle of*

*the loaves and fishes continues in providing for all these people through so many there, who I am sure, share our feeling of being so weak and inadequate in our love. It is the miracle of God's love working through our weakness. There is no other explanation. This is our secret."*

It is the secret of beauty repeatedly born out of darkness and of needs consistently met which marks the history of the Missionary Brothers. The Order itself was born of necessity for it arose from Mother Teresa's recognition that some aspects of her work were more suited to men than to women. Initially one or two priests tried working with the Sisters in the slums but Mother Teresa's plans were for something much more extensive. She was considering the possibility of a new foundation – a Congregation of Brothers, very similar to that of the Missionary Sisters of Charity, trained in the same spirit and working in conjunction with them. By 1963 there were a few candidates and the beginnings of a new branch of the Missionary Brothers of Charity was blessed by Archbishop Albert D'Souza but Rome did not at first approve the foundation. Recognition by Rome depended on large numbers but priests were understandably reluctant to send candidates to join the Brothers until they had become a recognised Institute. The earliest years of the Order were stunted by this delicate impasse, and the fact that the Roman Catholic Church does not permit a woman to be head of a religious Congregation of men presented a further difficulty. In 1964, however, the solution to this latter problem presented itself in the form of Father Ian Travers-Ball, an Australian Jesuit who was spending his tertianship at Sitagarha. To Mother Teresa it was something more than a beautiful coincidence that the Brothers began their work on the 25th March, 1963, the very day on which their future Superior was ordained a Jesuit priest in Hazaribagh.

Father Travers-Ball had always been interested in working for the poor and as an experiment during his tertianship he was sent for a few weeks to work with the Brothers residing in Shishu Bhavan. According to Mother Teresa, after that there was no question of what he should do. Like her, he received a call within a call. With permission he left the Jesuit Order to become Brother Andrew. The Brothers were entrusted to his care because, as Mother Teresa put it, "He is a very holy person. We are so different but both of us have the same mind." With careful explanation, the impasse with Rome was resolved, the Order of Brothers was given official approbation and in the course of time the candidates increased in number and the work spread.

The Missionary Brothers of Charity have no distinctive habit. They dress simply with only a cross pinned to their shirt or coat to distinguish them from those for whom they care. Some join as priests but in general no candidate is admitted specially for the priesthood for it is left to the Society to decide who will be sent to study for that particular calling. The fact that they do have priests among them, however, has allowed them to open houses in mission areas which until their arrival had no priest and no church. So it is that the Order, which now includes three hundred Brothers, has been able to open over thirty houses in ten countries.

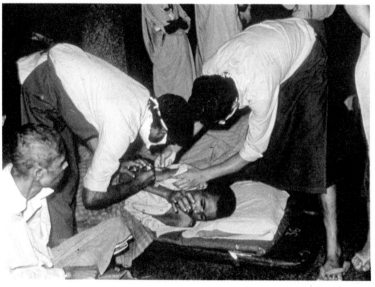

*In Nirmal Hriday, the Missionary Brothers dress the wounds of a man who might otherwise die alone on the streets.*

The Spirit of the Order is the same as that of the Missionary Sisters. They share a common spiritual director and, above all, a common conviction that the love they give to the suffering and the poor, they give for and to the Christ of St Matthew's Gospel. As a general policy the Brothers try not to go where the Sisters are already working, seeking instead those areas where those in need have been offered no glimpse of an infinite love, but the two Congregations do collaborate. They work together, for instance, in the Kalighat Home for the Dying where the Brothers look after the men while the Sisters care for the women, and at the Titagarh hospital for lepers, when the Sisters experienced some difficulty in dealing with the men, the Brothers took charge of the work there. There are certain differences in approach – "If anything, their training and their life is more arduous", one Sister Superior remarked with a laugh, "they think because they are men they can take it". Then more seriously she added, "They are very, very poor and very holy".

Their report for the year, 1979, however, betrays only the similarities of their work:

| | | | | |
|---|---|---|---|---|
| Brothers: Professed | 103 | Slum schools | | 35 |
| Novices | 67 | Number of children | | 4,442 |
| Postulants | 34 | | | |
| | | TB Centres | | 3 |
| Dying assisted | 2,876 | Number of patients | | 95 |
| For India only | | | | |
| | | Handicapped & mental | | |
| Catechism centres | 3 | patient centres | | 3 |
| Number of members | 45 | Number of patients | | 180 |
| | | | | |
| Mobile Clinics | 26 | Work programme | | |
| Number of patients | 17,000 | help | Several | |
| | | Number of persons | | 1,700 |
| Leprosy centres | 5 | | | |
| Number of patients | 10,000 | Commercial classes | | 2 |
| Also two leprosaria | | Boys and girls | | 65 |
| with 120 people | | | | |
| | | Feeding centres and | | |
| Leprosy Rehabilitation | | Medical help | | 8 |
| centres | 1 | Number of persons | | 4,500 |
| Number of patients | 25 | | | |
| | | Family food centres | | 5 |
| Home for Dying and | | Number of families | | 2,000 |
| Sick Destitutes | 3 | | | |
| Admissions | 320 | | | |
| | | | | |
| Home for Abandoned | | | | |
| Children | 5 | | | |
| Admissions (and three | | | | |
| orphans living with | | | | |
| Brothers) | 170 | | | |

The Brothers have twenty-one houses in India, five in the Far East (in Hong Kong, Taiwan, Japan, South Korea and Macao) and a further six in the Americas (three houses in Los Angeles, one in Santa Ana, one in San Salvador and one in Guatemala). They also have a contemplative branch in Rome.

Mansatala, the mother house of the Brothers in Calcutta provides a home not only for a small number of professed Brothers and a larger number of novices undergoing training, but also for twenty or so orphan boys whose upbringing is carefully supervised. Here also a meal for one thousand children is provided each day and a feeding centre is run for about fifty destitute leprosy patients. The house rents for one hundred families are provided each month and nearly five hundred families receive monthly rations of rice, Bulger or wheat, medicines and clothes.

In the village of Noynan, the Brothers have set up a centre for their village work. From here they care for five hundred poverty-stricken families, run a primary school where the children can attend classes and receive a daily meal, and treat patients suffering from T.B. in a home opened specifically for that purpose.

In Dum Dum the Brothers run a small radio training centre for handicapped boys in an attempt to equip these children for a future career and at the Pipe Road, Calcutta centre five professed Brothers share the upbringing of no less than thirty-five boys, who are without one or both parents and who, because they speak and write different languages, have to be dispatched to a number of different schools. On the overcrowded platforms of India's railway stations the Missionary Brothers attempt to carry a little love to children who have made the only home they know under a piece of discarded matting. One young English Co-Worker writes of his stay with the Brothers:

*"They go regularly to the railway stations in order to show the children that someone cares for them, they chat to them and make friends with them. One of the things they do is to take a bar of soap and make sure the boys wash themselves under the water towers which are used for filling up the engines for India still uses steam trains. The little boys – they may be any age from eight to fifteen – live on the stations and*

*make money whenever possible, by carrying suitcases for the passengers on the trains. Some of the boys are refugees from Bangladesh and some are homeless. They live in gangs where the eldest boy is generally the leader and looks after the young ones. The Brothers are always cheerful and always smiling."*

Outside India, the strife-ridden areas of S.E. Asia cried out desperately for a presence which was ever-cheerful and ever-smiling. In the early 1970s the Brothers went to Saigon as bearers of joy and found that in the midst of war and strife, they became the recipients of an unexpected warmth:

*"Let me describe our house here in Saigon",* writes one American Missionary Brother. *"The first floor sleeps about thirty or so of the shelterless people. The second floor is the same but has room for classes during the day. The third floor is for the Brothers. It consists of two small rooms in which we eat, sleep, read and pray. Each Brother has a sleeping pallet like the ones the people use and this is rolled up during the day. There is no privacy and always much noise. We feed over a hundred people a day in the house. The transition has been easy for me, thank God, although the hardest thing to accept is the rats. Rain has driven them indoors and we can hear and feel them running around the floor at night.*

*"We really live in underworld Saigon. Most Vietnamese have never even been down these streets. We live off an alley in which no more than two people can walk abreast at a time yet thousands of people must live in this alley. We can walk here at all hours in complete safety. The people know who we are and why we are here. They are all so good to us. The children are all so well behaved and share all they have with us. It's so touching to have a small child come up to you and offer you some of his bread.*

*"Our other houses in Saigon will be for the crippled, disabled and retarded who have no-one to care for them. One of our Brothers has medical experience and will guide us. I'm convinced that the Spirit of the Lord is here. He's given me the grace to make an early adjustment. And what a grace it is! I came to Asia, to confusion, and I find peace. I expect to find a war, and hate, and instead I find love. Instead of despair, the people have so much joy. And we share in their joy. It is good to be here."*

Remarkably it was the assistance and dedication of a former prostitute which enabled the work in Saigon to develop so effectively. One of many bar-girls and prostitutes whom Brother Andrew encountered while the country was still alive with foreign troops, the girl had been reduced to earning her living in this way after her husband had been killed by a stolen jeep driven by a drunken Australian civilian. She took to the streets in a desperate attempt to support her three small children and by the time the foreign soldiers began to withdraw she was more than ready to abandon the kind of life she had been leading. It was with her help that the Missionary Brothers were able to create a haven of stability at the heart of economic, emotional and political insecurity. With the pull-out of the Americans, jobs and money were scarce and many widows were left to struggle for their own and their children's survival against an all-enveloping tide of inflation. The aim was to provide a home for those poor who did not fit into the categories catered for by other organisations.

In 1975, however, the Communists took over the houses the Brothers had opened in Saigon and so forced them to abandon their mission. With no possibility of work, no hope of beginning anew and no place in which to live, Brother Andrew caught a plane for Bangkok and India. In his Christmas letter for that year he looks back with an aching heart:

*"This year has been heartbreaking. We lost five houses in Vietnam and Cambodia. The buildings don't matter. But to be separated so finally from all the people one came to know and love is unbelievably painful. I shall never be the same again after this, and I know that I shall have an ache in my heart for them until the day I die.*

*"The full story of the fall of Saigon and the change-over will never be told. The journalists who stayed on lived mostly in the downtown hotels. They did not penetrate the alleys and lanes of the overcrowded parts of the city. They did not really have the chance to share the feelings of the people I knew in Saigon in the reports of the media or in the general idea that people outside Vietnam have of what has been happening there.*

*"The story remains untold, and it will remain untold perhaps until the voice of some Vietnamese Solzhenitsyn is heard. But*

*if that ever happens, it will be after many years. As for myself, I don't have the heart to even attempt the telling.*
*"And so Vietnam and Cambodia is a closed book for me and the Brothers. And what unfolds there in the lives of the voiceless many in the coming years will not be known to us."*

Brother Andrew was experiencing the pain of birth and the anguish of the cross which he recognises with sadness in so many lives but which becomes the prelude to the "joyful life of Easter", for in a way which is unexpected and unplanned the pain, the sadness and the struggle is in some way taken up and made mysteriously fruitful.

In mid-summer of 1975, five Brothers, one Dutchman and four Americans who had served in the Order in South Vietnam and Cambodia until conditions had compelled them to leave, arrived in Los Angeles. In the Skid Row area of the city's downtown they found a tiny place to serve as their living quarters and as a house of prayer from which they could go out in search of Christ in the distressing disguise of his destitute and abandoned people. In the streets and alleys of Skid Row, they found him in those who had somehow fallen outside the scope of the giant welfare system and, above all in the men, women and children who, surrounded by materialism, remained unloved and estranged. From these encounters the Brothers were led into lonely hotel rooms, where in desperate isolation, the dignity of human life had been slowly neglected. They cleaned rooms filled with empty bottles or human excrement, they read to the blind, they accompanied the helpless to the large, sprawling complex of Los Angeles County Hospital, and they gently returned an old man living under cardboard in an alley to a nursing home from which he had escaped because he "found no love there".

Gradually young men began to join the Brothers in Los Angeles as "Come and Sees" – a term used by the Missionaries of Charity to describe those considering the life and work of the Order as a possible vocation. Brother Andrew, having left Vietnam, came to Los Angeles and in the midst of the city's intolerable suffering caused by an all too evident lack of love, he resolved to found a second novitiate. The spiritual formation of young men wishing to become Brothers from the Americas, Europe, Australia and New Zealand need not necessarily be undertaken in Calcutta.

*Production-centred Hong Kong has its own distinctive pressures, its own form of blindness and its own brand of poverty.*

112

They could be formed in the work and spirit of the Congregation in downtown Los Angeles. Another house was rented. As part of their formation, the novices were sent to work in the Skid Row area, visiting the old, the sick, the alcoholics and the neglected, trying to be a loving presence in a place where violence and alienation had become frighteningly ordinary. In both cities there were large numbers of people dying unwanted and neglected. There were the lepers – be they actual lepers or "social lepers" – such as the alcoholics and the street people; and there were the children, living under terrible conditions of physical or spiritual and emotional want. The work grew, the number of Brothers increased and homes of hospitality were opened for the homeless and those in need of emergency shelter, a shower, clean clothes, or simply a chat.

*"Sometimes",* writes Brother Andrew, *"we feel overwhelmed at how small our efforts are in relationship to the need. However, we can only try to keep in mind that we are simply the instruments God is using, and if we only let him, he can do marvellous things through these small communities of love. In his total plan then we need not worry about the numbers we can't reach, we need only be here, love here and believe that the good news of God's love will reach those most crushed, lonely and frightened.*
*"And here, where we encounter life in its most bruised and broken forms, we sometimes get a glimpse of the miracle of love in these very same lives. We are blessed to see the seemingly broken who are healed, the seeming sinner who is a saint, the seeming poor man who is rich in ways we could never imagine. Yes, God has blessed us. He brought us here today to witness the miracle of his presence born anew in the hearts of the poor. He is here among us, disguised in rags and dirt. It is he – hungry; it is he – thirsty; it is he – homeless and lonely. It is he, in Los Angeles, who walks the streets so disguised as even to be shocking to us."*

The same disguised Christ of universal love but universal need ensured the strengthening and expansion of the work carried out in his service. Los Angeles proved to be the starting point for new openings in Latin America. In the Far East more houses were established and work was begun in places such as Japan and Hong Kong. Plans have even been made to open in Europe, for experience has shown unforgettably that ostensibly prosperous societies have their own distinctive pressures, their own form of blindness and their own brand of poverty:

*"Sometimes people wonder why we go to more prosperous places like Los Angeles, Tokyo, Hong Kong, when there is such desperate poverty in India and on such a large scale. I believe that there is much more terrible poverty than that found in India. Hong Kong illustrates this for me. When I was in Calcutta recently during the floods which devastated so much, it struck me one day that the people of Calcutta are somehow much more humanly rich than people in Hong Kong. It is a strange paradox that may be saying something to us. It is true of much of the more affluent world. In Hong Kong we have a small home for severely mentally disabled men. We get public funds – and much interference. The men in the home are severely retarded. They have been in various institutions where they did not respond much to training or treatment. They lived with their families in the impossibly small rooms of Hong Kong housing conditions. Since joining us, all have responded well – and the big thing, it seems to me, is that they are happy. But that is not enough, we are told. They must be doing something, they must be programmed. There can be few places as rushed in the world as production-centred Hong Kong. The stress and pressures here are great. It seems we are not allowed to be satisfied that these disabled men are happy. They have to be got into the rush, into the rat-race that is driving everybody else mad. There are basic questions involved in this about where the dignity and value of a man lies, whether it is in his being or in his performance. And so India with its greater material poverty has a quality of life that is often lost when the gods are materialistic and must be got down in a report. It is a question of the human and spiritual enjoyment of life. I feel, in places like Hong Kong, we are meant to be a little witness to this as 'Animal Farm' bears down on all sides."*

The uncertainty of the world as economic crises grow steadily worse, political conflicts impress themselves increasingly on the lives of individuals and the young seek a restless escape in the nothingness of drugs, violence and permissive self-indulgence, exerts tremendous and to some intolerable pressures. Yet Brother Andrew is able to discern in all this, a constructive message:

*"Have faith in the Lord of History for there is nothing else that is certain or solid. Everything may collapse, and one may find oneself trapped in some falling or fallen city with all escapes gone. Then one would be finally poor – and free. There stands forever God's love and kindness and in a real extreme, one is aware of that . . . aware that there is only that."*

From the shadow of breakdown, from powerlessness in the face of the powers that be or strive to be, springs the need to focus on a God of consistent love who remains apparent in smallness and vulnerability. To counteract all that is destructive and temporary there are always the unidentified, unknown saints and the immeasurable greatness of the acts of so many hidden people. All that is so frequently lacking is the capacity to see and to value them, for the ability to see is often dependent on the upset of thinking impeded by a lifetime of conditioning processes and preconceived ideas.

Brother Andrew is by no means reluctant to regard what he describes as "a multi-purpose, five minute seminar from a child" as a great gift:

*"He was a little boy of about seven years, who had been brought to our Home for the Dying in Howrah. He was dying – but with simple care he recovered and was a very lively little boy when I met him playing around the home till we could find some better place for him. I was staying there, and for two days noticed that he always had with him a cheap rubber ball that he'd been given at a Christmas party. That ball was all he had in the world apart from the clothes he wore. In the evening he came up onto the terrace (where he shouldn't have been), with the ball of course, and he and I began to play with it. After a few minutes it bounced over the hedge, and he sped downstairs to recover it. Watching from the roof, I saw an older boy, a bit slow of mind, grab it and when the little boy arrived, he threw it over the wall. The little boy scaled the wall, couldn't find it, and then looked up at me who was thinking what a tragedy this loss was for him! But what he did was a gesture of 'It doesn't matter', scaled back over the wall, and went off with a carefree skip and a song. And I was left on the terrace to reflect on poverty of spirit,*

116

*Self-sufficiency means independence and dignity. It is for this reason that the Missionaries of Charity endeavour wherever possible to provide those in their care with some form of useful occupation.*

the Beatitudes, true freedom, and just who is rich and who is poor.

"*Maybe I'm crazy*", comments Brother Andrew, "*but after all these years close to desperately poor people, I strongly believe that the greatest pain is not found in Calcutta or Cambodia, or El Salvador or Siberia. In these places it is the hungry belly, the sick body, the wretchedly housed family. And while we work at these points of suffering, we make an enormous mistake if we fail to recognise the richness of spirit of the people of these places and situations.*"

The child's reaction was indeed remarkable; the lesson it teaches and its full implications belie a common assumption; but perhaps no less remarkable is the capacity to recognise

117

the real significance of a simple act on the part of a boy who is poor yet rich in spirit.

*"Christ tells us poor weary old adults of the world, with our heads full of books or business or science or the problems of the world, to learn from the little children and become more like them."*

So writes Brother Andrew and his words almost inevitably call to mind the story of Anna recorded by Fynn in "Mister God, this is Anna". At the age of six, Anna was a gardener, a mathematician, a poet, a philosopher and a theologian capable of bypassing all the non-essentials and distilling centuries of learning into a single sentence, "God said love me, love them, and love it and don't forget to love yourself." "According to her", writes Fynn, "each and every individual was issued at birth with various bits of glass labelled 'Good, Bad, Nasty', etc. People got in the habit of slipping these bits of glass over their inward eye and seeing things according to the colour and label of the glass. This we did", she gave Fynn to understand, "in order to justify our inner convictions".

Anna with the unimpeded vision of a child was able to perceive God in everything, for to her even the definition, "God is love", was too restrictive for a God, upon whom for centuries the world had attempted to impose human attributes, and with them human limitations, but who to her free-thinking spirit, quite patently defied all such restrictions. Brother Andrew puts it slightly differently, "So much of our way of judging is worldly – worldly in the sense that it doesn't get beyond what our heads can reason and plan", but the message is the same and it is one securely rooted in the Gospels – "Truly, I say to you, whoever does not receive the Kingdom of God like a child shall not enter it".

From the readiness to accept the overthrow or reversal of "conventional" standards of judgement there comes a glimmer of understanding of that deep paradoxical mystery of life which determines that it is the meek who will inherit the earth, it is the last who will be first and the poor who will enter the Kingdom of Heaven. So it is that Brother Andrew is able to perceive that Kingdom in the middle of a turbulence that is well and truly "earthed":

*"As I travel around many countries with all the problems,*

*suffering, violence and evil. I see one thing very clearly. It is that everywhere there are small hidden souls whose hearts are true and good and full of love. These are not the ones who make the headlines, but they are the life and hope of the world.*

*"I think of Odilia, a young girl in Korea, who has been coming to our house in Seoul for nearly three years almost every evening after her work to help with the cooking, and who always has time for a bright word and smile for the most overlooked of the old and disabled men living with us.*

*"I think of our ambulance driver in Calcutta who in his old age still works to support his family who should really be supporting him now, and who has a devotion and a faithfulness that shames most of our Brothers."*

He remembers too a boy "with a stiff leg and something missing from his mind":

*"The Sisters had found him on the streets, and he said, 'My name is Johnny Walker' — a name he or we never changed. He was thrown out as a child, crippled, low IQ, couldn't learn to read. And yet he was so joyful and happy always, ever ready with a funny song or dance to bring joy to others. He made others with sad stories laugh and forget. He would pray each day with the other boys and came to mass on Sundays. He would join his hands and bow his head. He knew that God was present and he knew that love and joy and a smile are at the heart of God.*

*"So Johnny died at eighteen, drowned in a few inches of water, when he had an unexpected fit. Now he is a saint — after a joyfully successful life if ever there was one."*

Then there was the little nameless Vietnamese girl who would have had plenty of reason to be worried and anxious if she had sat down to consider her history and her prospects but who skipped down the stairs of the Brothers' house in Vietnam with a happy song on her lips.

*"And there are countless others",* continues Brother Andrew. *"They don't do big things. They suffer the injustices of the world without bitterness or anger",* and here again it would appear there is a lesson to be learned. *"They are not only the blessed of the Kingdom of Heaven that Jesus spoke of. They are also the saviour and liberators with Christ*

*for the likes of myself who need them.*

*"The Gospel of Christ is full of contradictions to our worldly way of thinking. One night in May I was returning to Calcutta from Ranchi. While I was on the platform another train pulled in, and a crowd of poor tribal people clambered out carrying heavy bundles of firewood to sell — men, women, old and young. They cut the wood in the mountains, carry it to their villages, cut it to size, tie it, and carry it again a long way to the nearest railway station. Then they battle into the crowded train with it. It is hard and heavy work. They are harassed by forest guards, police, the railways. Finally they sell it in the city for next to nothing. After arriving at the Ranchi station they sleep for the night on the platform and sell their wood in the morning to the merchants.*

*"You would expect such people to be sad and oppressed. But on that hot summer's night, as they climbed up from the tracks onto the platform with their heavy bundles, as they lay down tired for the night, or ate the food of the poor, or smoked a cigarette, there was a laughter, a joking, a contentment, a fellowship that the richer ones of the world may well envy and that might make the reformers and revolutionaries pause to reflect on what they might transform these people into. One of the tragic results of much political activism that aims at justice is the bitterness and hatred that it succeeds in putting into the hearts of the poor of the world. It is not an improvement. It is not liberation. There must be joy in our projects and our causes. Otherwise we have not found the Spirit of Christ. Thus spoke those simple tribal folk to me on that hot steamy night."*

To Brother Andrew, it would seem, the presence of God is identifiable even in the small, the unknown and the hidden, and the clue to its detection remains irrepressibly, joy.

# CHAPTER SIX

# THE CO-WORKERS

Into the bosom of the one great sea
Flow streams that come from hills on every side,
Their names are various as their springs,
And thus in every land do men bow down
To one great God, though known by many names.

A SOUTH INDIAN FOLKSONG

"It all began really when I was heavily pregnant", remarked the International Chairman of the Co-Workers of Mother Teresa. The history of the Co-Workers promised to be yet another example of the extraordinary presented and almost dismissed as the mundane and the fragile.

"I had been working with others in a shop called 'The Good Companions' in Calcutta, selling handiwork in aid of the missions until I became too pregnant and had to hand in my notice. One afternoon I was sitting on the balcony in the heat, wondering what on earth I could do and suddenly it just came to me – I would find Mother Teresa. I had never met her but I had read the occasional notice in the newspaper and I knew that a friend of mine had a vague connection with her." So it was that on 26th July, 1954 Mrs Ann Blaikie went with the friend in question to Mother Teresa's first clinic. Mother Teresa took them with her to the Kalighat and in the car en route they offered to collect toys for the annual Christmas party about which they had read in the Calcutta press. Mother Teresa, delighted, asked them if they would be able to raise enough money to buy dresses or shirts and shoes for her Christian children at Christmas. With great enthusiasm a dozen European women made angels out of tin foil and beads and sold them to raise the necessary funds. At Christmas the slum children were provided with the clothes they so desperately needed and given old toys which had been meticulously painted up. "After Christmas", one of these very earliest Co-Workers recalls, "we gathered together with something of an air of self-congratulation and waited for Mother Teresa to come and thank us. This she did but added that she now needed clothes and presents for the Muslim children's annual festival. Somehow we knew that the Hindu children's party must inevitably follow." Mother Teresa's call for more than a passing and superficial commitment was already impressing itself upon them.

Because this group of well-wishers had begun its work in Marian Year it became known as the Marian Society. Its efforts were not initially directed exclusively towards helping Mother Teresa but included the support of other missions. Gradually the Society expanded to include Indians and Anglo-Indians and to incorporate some who were not Roman Catholics, and the work done to assist Mother Teresa increased in scope. Groups of women formed working parties to roll bandages out of old sheets and to make paper bags out of newspaper in which the leper pills could be more easily distributed. As the leprosy work developed it was the future international chairman of the Co-Workers who took over the organisation of the flag-days and the appeals which made the early clinics possible, and it was a future national link for the Sick and Suffering Co-Workers who designed the stickers appealing to those in a position to give to touch a leper with their compassion, and who with some difficulty contrived to produce a letter heading which at Mother Teresa's express request made India the centre of the world. Christmas cards were made and sold in aid of the work and food and blankets were collected for distribution to the lepers.

*The insignia for the Missionaries of Charity was designed in 1961 and presented to Mother Teresa.*

All this was of course highly commendable, but was it not simply what Mother Teresa might describe as "giving from an abundance"? Did it not represent an attempt by well-meaning but well-to-do people to salve their consciences in a small and relatively comfortable way? One Co-Worker looks back with unjustified self-reproach on her own efforts and her own reactions when in the home for the dying, she actually came inescapably face to face with poverty and suffering: "There were we living, really in great style with all these servants. Somehow, it is a terrible thing to say, but one does become immune to poverty which is so extreme... and there all around you, all the time. The home for the dying was a strange twilight world. For me there was a touch of unreality about it all. In Shishu Bhavan too, everything was spotlessly clean and of course the work was wonderful but in those early days everything was terribly primitive." The admission betrays a rare honesty and a gentle reminder of the ever present danger of romanticising the extraordinary and so reducing it to the ordinary. Remarkable things have happened in the home for the dying; some have described it

**MOTHER TERESA APPEALS**
TO THE
**CHILDREN OF BRITAIN**

2d. buys a slice of bread for a hungry child in India. **How many slices will you give each week?**

THE CHILDREN OF DENMARK GIVE A MUG OF MILK EACH. PLEASE GIVE THE COST OF A **SLICE OF BREAD** TO EAT WITH IT.

DONATIONS TO—
FEED THE CHILDREN FUND
MOTHER TERESA COMMITTEE
**E. P. TATLOCK,**
**8 MISTLEY COURT,**
**ASHLEY ROAD,**
**EPSOM, SURREY.**

THE L–S PRESS LTD., WALTON-ON-THAMES

CO-WORKERS OF MOTHER TERESA

**WORLD CHILD WELFARE FUND**

Hon. Treasurer
World Child Welfare Fund
11 Basing Close
Thames Ditton
Surrey KT7 0HY

*In the early days when fund raising was necessary, appeals in England rallied support for the homeless and hungry children of India.*

as the "most wonderful place on earth", many have found themselves able to overcome all fears and reservations and to respond in a way that they would never have imagined possible. Mother Teresa delights in telling the story of a young girl from Mauritius who joined the Order. One of the first places to which the new novices are sent is the Home for the Dying. When this young woman returned to the Convent after her first visit, Mother Teresa met her and, seeing her radiant face, asked her why she was so happy? "Oh Mother", was the girl's reply, "I have been touching the body of Christ for three hours". It is doubtless true to suggest, however, that it is not given to everyone to react in this way so immediately and with such apparent ease.

In the early days of the Marian Society tasks were allocated according to talents and abilities and when Mother Teresa felt individual members understood enough about her teaching they worked beside the Sisters in the schools or the clinics. Some continued in the working parties. Others helped in Shishu Bhavan or in Nirmal Hriday. What was of vital importance was that the work, whatever form it took, was an expression of something more than simple humanitarian concern. Another of the early Co-Workers remembers working in the children's home. "Mother Teresa would visit Shishu Bhavan every morning. She would go from one baby to the next and if she spotted one which was so frail and so sick that it would obviously die that day, she would wrap it in a blanket and give it to one of the helpers to hold with the instruction to love that child until it died. What

*What was of vital importance was that the work, whatever form it took, was an expression of something more than simple humanitarian concern.*

124

mattered was that no child in her care should have died without having experienced love. I remember one morning Mother Teresa put one of these desperately sick babies into my arms and I held it and loved it until it finally died at 6 o'clock in the evening. I passed away the hours by humming Brahms' lullaby and do you know, I could feel that baby, tiny and weak as it was, press itself against me."

The same Co-Worker remembers her first visit to Nirmal Hriday: "From Shishu Bhavan, Mother Teresa would go on to the Home for the Dying, taking one or two helpers with her to work amongst the dying. The first time I went, I walked there alone with Mother Teresa. She must have sensed that I was nervous and apprehensive because before we arrived she stopped and said to me, 'I don't want you to go to the home for the dying feeling sad. Pray and ask God to lift up your heart because whatever you see there, I want you to transmit joy.' "

Much was asked of those who wished to help and in various and sometimes very personal ways much was given. Another early recollection of Shishu Bhavan demonstrates with simple poignancy how effective this giving was. One of the helpers in the home, who had left her work there temporarily to have a baby, returned with her new-born son to be greeted with great excitement and anticipation by the children of Shishu Bhavan. They were told that if they sat down quietly they could each hold the baby. Accordingly they sat down in a circle and the baby was passed from one pair of eagerly outstretched hands to the next until it reached one Indian child who sat with his hands firmly clasped behind his back. When asked why he would not hold the baby the boy replied with obvious distress, "he is so pale, he must be very ill". It had never for one moment entered the child's head that the Co-Worker was white, European and not one of them.

Other lay people began to offer their services. Doctors, nurses and dentists volunteered to staff Mother Teresa's clinics and treated her children in their own surgeries free of charge. A Jewish doctor offered to operate on any children suffering from hare lips and cleft palates and himself paid for their hospitalisation. Students from the university went on Saturdays to shave the dying men in Nirmal Hriday and at Christmas volunteers filled paper bags with gifts for the children. Women went to the convent to teach the Indian Sisters English, the language of the Order and most remarkable of all, a high caste Hindu lady, resplendent in a silk sari, went regularly to wash the dying and tend the sick, a task which would have been utterly inconceivable to her parents in the days when the poor were untouchable, and a Bearer would have been called to dust a chair if the shadow of one of these suffering people had so much as fallen upon it.

Of the early European helpers, who had been prepared if necessary to spend their time searching for new centres in the monsoon mud, a number returned to England in 1960. Remarkably they all settled in Surrey within ten miles of each other and within a week of her arrival in England Ann Blaikie was once more caught up in the work of Mother Teresa. John Southworth, the chairman of a leprosy relief charity had been sending money to Mother Teresa for her work amongst the lepers and she advised him to contact her friend in England for up-to-date information on the situation in India. The outcome was almost inevitable. Some six months later Mother Teresa visited London and gave a television appearance. From the offers of help which followed, what was then called the Mother Teresa Committee was born, under the chairmanship of John Southworth, the vice-chairmanship of Ann Blaikie and with the support of other friends from India.

The focal point of the activities of these first UK helpers was a monthly meeting which began and ended with prayer and meditation and which also devoted itself to organising material help for the Missionaries of Charity. Under the Child Welfare Scheme donors agreed to sponsor one of the orphaned or abandoned children in the care of the Sisters. People were encouraged to make bandages from old linen, to knit blankets and to collect used clothing. Items suitable for India were sent to a number of collecting centres throughout the country and dispatched to Calcutta for use in the Homes for the Dying, clinics and children's homes, through the kind offices of "Help the Aged" and "War on Want". Each year newly designed Christmas cards were sent out to friends or placed on sale at the mission for the Relief of Suffering shop in Knightsbridge. A sample medicine scheme sent free samples of medicine to the clinics where the need for them was so overwhelmingly great, and money was raised through the collection and sale of used stamps and through other similar enterprises. A newsletter was published at regular intervals to keep those interested in touch with current activities and news from India, and a limited amount of advertising was undertaken in those early years, but the principal way in which these helpers sought to enlarge their circle of members was through talks (illustrated by a film or slides) to schools and other organisations. Every encouragement was given to people living in different parts of the country to form groups of their own, and so as in India so in England the number of "men of good will" increased steadily. The pattern for development in other countries was already set.

*The letter heading for the Missionaries of Charity and the Co-Workers still makes India the centre of a world encircled by a rosary.*

When Mother Teresa conceived the idea of an Association of helpers committed to assisting the Missionaries of Charity, she chose for them the name of Co-Workers, an expression applied by Mahatma Ghandhi to his own helpers who worked with him, as he put it, "for the brotherhood of man under the fatherhood of God". The term is a graceful tribute to the man who found his ideal of service in the words of Krishna: "The man who casts off all desires and walks without desire, with no thought of a mine and an I, comes into peace", and who made the plight of the "pariah" or untouchables his personal concern. His own impulse to share the life of those who struggled on the very lowest rung of the Hindu caste system – "I do not want to be reborn but if I have to be reborn, I should be born an untouchable, so that I may share their sorrows, sufferings and affronts levelled at them, in order that I may endeavour to free myself and them from that miserable condition" – finds an unmistakable echo in Mother Teresa's identification with the poorest of the poor; and the principles inextricably associated with his term, Co-Worker, namely those of service, love and universality under God, have proved to be an exceptionally appropriate inspiration to the now international Co-Workers of Mother Teresa.

Even the very first pioneers who would later tell others from their own experience, of the work of love being carried out in the slums of India, were of many different nationalities and creeds. If all were to be united in one Association, then the constitution must be acceptable not to any one country or any one faith but to all, and based on the united, and in itself unifying recognition that through service to the poor an individual can come to love God better. "So it was in order to draw up a Constitution for these Co-Workers," their international chairman remembers, "that Mother Teresa called us to Rome in March, 1969. For two whole days we wrestled with the draft, keeping before us always this spirit of love and service which has inspired the Missionaries of Charity; we had to remember that Co-Workers were not necessarily Christian, indeed, Mother Teresa once estimated that for every Christian in India who helped her she had nine non-Christians helping. So we had to word our Constitution to appeal to men of good will everywhere, to Hindus, Buddhists, Pagans or Christians. We had to consider also the social barriers which divide Co-Workers in some parts of the world – the very rich and the poor who would not necessarily work together in acts of charity, but who could be helped to do so by a charismatic Constitution. Mother Teresa has affiliated the Association to her own Missionaries of Charity, surely the first time that an Association of lay, not primarily Christian people, has been associated to a Religious Order."

The difficulties proved to be by no means insuperable. On 26th March the Constitution of the International Association of Co-Workers of Mother Teresa was presented to Pope Paul VI and received his blessing. In a letter of acknowledgement, Cardinal Agagianian, head of the Sacred Congregation of the Propagation of the Faith at the Vatican praised the ideal of the newly-formed Association: "This Sacred Congregation commends most highly the ideal which the Association offers to its members, namely, union in prayer and sacrifice to the good works of your Institute and wholehearted free service to the poorest of the poor of all castes and creeds.

Adherence to the Constitution, drawn up in Rome effected a unique bond between Co-Workers throughout the world. Those who during the floods of 1968, for example, worked beside the Sisters in the foothills of the Himalayas, among the former inhabitants of a town submerged beneath six feet of silt, mud and water, were mysteriously but effectively linked with those who in England quietly raised money for ambulance clinics to be shipped out to India. The woman who amongst the affluence of Cobham set up the "Teresa Boutique", a charity shop, selling nearly-new clothes, knitted garments and dolls to support the work of Mother Teresa shared a common bond with those who, at the very heart of the turmoil, endeavoured to ensure that the Missionaries of Charity need not turn away a single refugee from East Pakistan because of lack of resources; and eventually with countless others throughout the world who shared what was to be called "the Co-Workers Way of Life".

Today there are branches of the International Association of Co-Workers in all of the following countries:

| | | |
|---|---|---|
| Australia | Ireland | Peru |
| Austria | Italy | Philippines |
| Belgium | Japan | Singapore |
| Brazil | Luxembourg | Spain |
| Canada | Malta | Sweden |
| Denmark | Mauritius | Switzerland |
| France | Mexico | United States |
| Germany | Netherlands | Venezuela |
| Great Britain | New Zealand | Yugoslavia |
| India | Panama | |

There are also individual Co-Workers in Finland, Gibraltar, East Germany, Hungary, Poland, Czechoslovakia and Russia and there are even Eskimo Co-Workers in the icy reaches of the Arctic Circle. The wide distribution of members of the Association conjures up the apparently inevitable image of a huge and complex international organisation. Yet Mother Teresa has repeatedly stressed that the hundreds of thousands of Co-Workers scattered over five continents are members not of an "organisation" in the ordinary sense of the word but rather of a family united in the desire to come closer to God and to each other through prayer and loving service to their fellow men.

The Co-Workers are committed to uniting their lives progressively with the work of Mother Teresa and the Missionaries of Charity, and part of that commitment involves the supply of material goods to meet the needs which the Missionaries of Charity encounter in their service to the poor. As that service has increased in scope and volume so the need for clothes, food, medicine and equipment has increased accordingly, and so the amount of organisation involved, the sums of money required have also grown considerably. A single list issued to Co-Workers of the requirements of the Missionaries of Charity in India alone gives some idea of the nature of the need:

**Medicines for common ailments:**
Antiseptic creams of any kind
Medicines for dysentery and diarrhoea
Purgatives – (not suppositories)
Medicines for coughs, colds, bronchitis
Vitamins – very important – of any kind
T B medicines
Tonics
Antibiotics which are not time-barred, ie not within one year
Antibiotic ointment or cream or drops for eyes, nose
Leprosy pills

**Equipment for Clinics:**
Kidney bowls    Trays    Needles    Syringes

**Food for Clinics**
Complan,  Horlicks,  Condensed milk   Tinned baby foods

**Clothes**
a)   Anything serviceable – sorted and with a list of contents on the outside of each bale
b)   All white clothes, ie vests, aprons, sheets. Anything white should be parcelled separately for the use of the Sisters

or Brothers or for the Missionaries of Charity
c)   Cut pieces of material can be included in parcels but not sent separately, because they then become liable for duty
d)   Sandals are suitable for inclusion in bales
e)   Nylon clothes are also acceptable

*Not* heavy coats, boots, shoes, handbags, evening attire

Also – always wanted
    Bandages (made from torn sheets)
    Nylon stockings and tights (used for bandaging the stumps of lepers and numerous other purposes)
    Blankets (especially cot size)

This list is by no means a complete record of the items which pass unobtrusively over the thousands of miles which sometimes separate the Co-Workers from the readily identifiable "poorest of the poor" of the "Third World". It is simply one of many requests for material help which the Co-Workers have offered to meet and the quantity of goods actually supplied (in 1979, 2,194 bales were shipped from Great Britain alone; one million tablets of Dapsone are dispatched monthly) is a striking tribute to their achievements. So great a volume of materials cannot be handled without some degree of organisation. Goods must be assembled, sorted, transported and deposited at the docks in such a condition that bales destined for India can be fumigated in accordance with trade stipulations. Accounts must be properly kept and audited, trade agreements must be scrutinised and legal requirements must be met. The need for professional skills is apparently endless and the need for central co-ordination of all these skills is inescapably obvious.

The danger of funds intended to alleviate suffering becoming absorbed and emasculated by the supporting system and of that very system operating for its own sake is one which has threatened most charitable organisations and one of which Mother Teresa has been deeply and ever increasingly aware. If Mother Teresa is in Calcutta, then there is always a strong possibility that she will answer any

*A letter from Mother Teresa overleaf pinpoints the basis of what she insists is not an organisation but a family.*

Missionaries of Charity.
54A, Lower Circular Road,
Calcutta-16.
29/2/76

My dear Co-workers.

God love you for all
the love you have given;
for all the care you have
taken, for all the beautiful
lives you have lived - in
your own homes and you
neighbours.

This year we are going
to try very specially to grow
in Silence - that we may
pray better.
in Kindness - that we may
love each other as He loves (me)
in humility - that we
may become holy and

fulfill the reason for our existence – for we have been created for greater things – to be holy. Holiness is not the luxury of the few but a simple duty for you and for me to let us be holy as our Father in Heaven is Holy.

Each one of you are in my prayer – let us all together – do every thing in our power – to make our homes a place of peace, joy and love.

God bless you

M. Teresa

incoming telephone calls herself. Her work amongst the poor and the sick has remained unaltered. The fact that she has been the recipient of some of the world's highest accolades, the companion of statesmen and princes, has by no means removed her to the unattainable reaches of a hierarchy which would separate her from those to whose service she has committed her entire life. Every hour absorbed by the few demands of public life to which she allows herself to be subjected, is in her heart of hearts resented because it is detracting her from those all-consuming works of love. This is the spirit with which she tries to imbue her Co-Workers and the direction is all the more effective because she asks of others nothing that she has not been and is not still prepared to do herself. The message proclaims itself repeatedly: action, whatever form it takes, must not be action for its own sake but a manifestation of faith and love, carefully and constantly maintained in that perspective. Over the years her insistence that she does not want the work to become a business but to remain a work of love, a witness to trust in Divine Providence, has become if anything more emphatic. In particular, the fund-raising which was recognised as necessary in the early days has in more recent years been banned:

*"I want to make it very clear I do not want our Co-Workers to be involved in fund raising. It was necessary before for us to have Flag Days, Leper Days, Children's Days and all this. We had to do all this because nobody knew we existed but now the work has involved so many people that we just get – even in India where we never need to get anything before – we used to get about 20,000 after working hours and hours – those who were in Calcutta they know how hard they had to work – now without even asking, without any difficulties we get quite a lot of money and help for the lepers. "Let us avoid publicity under that fund raising name" she continues, "because it has become like a target with other organisations and people are beginning to doubt and so let us not give them a chance".*

Money given to the Missionaries of Charity is dealt with as effectively and simply as possible. Since money sent to India cannot be taken out of the country again, all finances not earmarked for India or specifically allocated to some other country are dealt with in Rome. Only Mother Teresa can authorise the disposition of funds in these two places. Once the Sisters are established in any one country Mother Teresa withdraws all financial support for they are expected to become independent, responsible for their own upkeep and for works in their own neighbourhood. The Co-Workers' money is handled similarly in India or Rome. They are, however, entitled to take some money out of the funds and to deposit it in a bank to earn interest for expenses only. The capital is then sent on. In this way Mother Teresa can guarantee that all money given goes to her work.

*Expenses are kept to a minimum. Clothing and other items for distribution are stored in an assembly of old crates.*

"Expenses" must be kept to a minimum. Co-Workers have no offices and no paid help anywhere in the world. Ambulances are no longer bought in England and shipped out to India because there are cheaper methods of achieving the same end. The newsletter which began its life as a glossy pamphlet is now a simple, unembellished typed sheet, the printing of other information sheets has been cut in the interests of "utmost economy" and "Inter Co-Worker Communication" is undertaken not on the official headed notepaper but on a motley selection of scraps of old paper guaranteed to baffle those unfamiliar with the system. Collecting centres, despite the apparent grandeur of the name, generally consist of a private garage, a vacant cellar, an unused corner of a church hall or simply "somebody's spare room". Transport entails virtually any available means of locomotion which is cheap or free, including the backs of lorries driven by well-intentioned drivers heading for city markets or the docks. Essential professional services are provided almost entirely by the free and miscellaneous talents of willing Co-Workers which guarantee no shortage of qualified advice and which have meant, for example, that the Liverpool home for women can boast its very own doctor, dentist and psychiatrist, all of whom as Co-Workers give of their time and skills free of charge. The system is orientated towards voluntary help by a refreshing readiness to accept the unconventional and by its flexibility. When through one contact special concessions were made available for shipping between Belgium and South America, for instance, there was no question of Belgian Co-Workers not assuming a special concern for the requisites of the Missionaries of Charity in South America.

Items donated, which are of no direct use to the Missionaries of Charity are happily passed on to other organisations or individuals who may make better use of them. The whole amounts to a free flow of materials, ideas and energies which is somewhat miraculously watched over by a series of committees and chairmen operative at regional, national and international levels and if there is a danger of those involved losing sight of the direction and purpose of their function, the instructions of Mother Teresa form a constant reminder:

*"We must not drift away from the humble works, because these are the works nobody will do. It is never too small. We are so small we look at things in a small way. But God, being Almighty, sees everything great. Therefore, even if you write a letter for the blind man, or you just go and sit and listen, or you take the mail for them, or you visit somebody or bring a flower to somebody – small things – or wash clothes for somebody or clean the house.*
*"Very humble work, that is where you and I must be. For there are many people who can do big things. But there are very few people who will do the small things. It is the small things that Sisters and Brothers do. We can do very little for the people, but at least they know that we do love them and that we care for them and that we are at their disposal."*

Mother Teresa is by no means alone in her concentration on humble work. For a variety of reasons many have chosen to focus on small acts of love or generosity, not least of them the playwright and poet, Bertolt Brecht who took as the inspiration for his poem, "Die Nachtschalter" an action which to Mother Teresa might well qualify as "beautiful":

*I hear that during the winter months in New York,*
*A man stands on the corner of 26th Street and Broadway*
*every evening*
*And begs a place for the night for the homeless*
*who gather there*
*By asking those who pass by.*

*The world is not changed in this way*
*The relationships between men do not improve*
*The age of exploitation is not shortened in this way.*
*But a few men have a place for the night*
*They are sheltered from the wind for one night*
*The snow intended for them falls on the street.*

In the final verse, however, the poet's message moves beyond the scope of what Mother Teresa sees as her mission and that of the Co-Workers.

*Don't put the book down, You, Man, who are reading it.*
*A few men have a place for the night*
*They are sheltered from the wind for one night*
*The snow intended for them falls on the street.*
*But the world is not changed in this way*
*The relationships between men are not improved in this way*
*The age of exploitation is not shortened in this way.*

Brecht was urging the overthrow of a corrupt capitalist society, of the system which he held responsible for the deprivation and suffering of those who were dependent on the charity of others even for something so fundamental as a night shelter. To him the action of the man on the corner of 26th Street and Broadway, however laudable it might appear, paled into insignificance in the light of the enormity of the need to change economic and social structures. As a drop in the ocean which should not be allowed to appease the pangs of social conscience, it is almost belittled. There have of course been those who have attempted to put this kind of

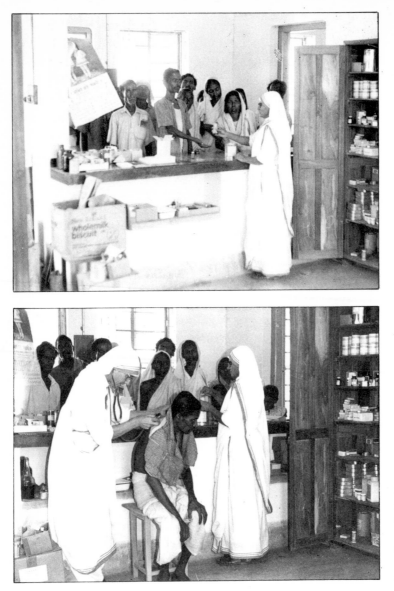

*The early clinics where medicines were sorted into general categories, labelled "head-aches", "stomach-aches" etc and stored in cigarette tins, were remarkable for their simple efficiency.*

reasoning to Mother Teresa, those who have suggested that by teaching their members resignation and passivity instead of revolution which strikes at social structures, religious leaders make themselves partly responsible for the poverty about which they profess to be concerned, and that concern for the collective, rather than the individual would achieve greater results. To Mother Teresa, the mission of love which she acknowledges to be but a drop in the ocean, can never be considered useless for without that drop, the ocean would be even smaller: "There are in the world those who struggle for justice and for human rights and try to change structures. We are not inattentive to this, but our daily contact is with men who do not even have a piece of bread to eat. Our mission is to look at the problem more individually. If a person feels that God wants him to pledge for the collective change of the social structures this is a question between him and God."

Her revolution she states emphatically "comes from God and is made by love" and in the course of a revolution of this kind there is no time and no real way to evaluate concrete results. She does not agree that religion makes men more passive and resigned. "In India, for example, this does not happen. Indians believe that their poverty is a reparation for the harm that they did in a previous incarnation but they are not passive. They have a certain conformity – conformity similar to that which Jesus showed during his passion. I saw in Algados things which I did not see at all in India, just as in India I meet things which I do not encounter anywhere else. The religions are not to be blamed for this situation. More and more we need to learn from the beautiful that is in every-thing – even in a poor person who is able to pass days without eating. Would we have this capacity? They are a people full of life, who incredible as it seems, smile, have hopes, who are able to lead a life purer than ours and for this are nearer to God. The beauty is not in poverty but in the courage that they show by still smiling and having hope."

For this reason Mother Teresa cannot condone the actions of those who attempt to instil bitterness into the hearts of individuals who are in reality already free, happy and without the aggression of those who aspire or can aspire to many things. "The persons who try to raise in these very poor a sense of aggression, violence, hostility against the governments – these persons do not understand the harm that they do because they withdraw from these poor the rich-ness of joy, of fullness. These persons who make use of these poor to arm revolutions do a great harm." Asked what ideology she considered to be in the best interests of the poor, her reply, unintentionally perhaps, makes a mockery of such intellectual abstractions. "The very poor do not need words but actions and I have not the conditions to analyse systems, economic patterns, ideologies. I recognise that each person has a conscience and must attend to its calling. Mine is this. Many times they already told me that I must not offer fishes to men, but rods so that they can fish themselves. Ah! My

God! Many times they do not have the strength to hold the rods . . . Giving them fishes, I help them to recover the strength for the fishing of tomorrow" . . . "To know the problem of poverty, intellectually is not to understand it as a problem. It is not through reading, taking a walk in the slums, admiring and regretting the misery that we get to understand it and to discover what of it is bad and good. We have to dive into it, to live it and to share it." The words of a woman whose life has been repeatedly identified as faith at its most articulate and convincing – namely in action, defy contradiction.

The man on the corner of 26th Street and Broadway has been placed in a very different perspective for by an action which rationally, in relation to the enormity and the horror of the need is perhaps negligible, he has demonstrated something more than simple humanitarian concern for an abstract ideal of justice or for the anonymous faceless mass of the distant poor. Instead he has put into action a concrete and immediate love for the human person. In an age where there is a tendency to confuse Christian love with political, economic and social preoccupations and to substitute categories of race, class, creed and colour for the unique identity of the individual, Mother Teresa insists that this love should reach beyond the accidental and the exterior barriers of ethnic origin, physical appearance, social status or intellectual achievement to the unique and personal root of each human being which is a part of God present in every individual created in his own image. It is the magnitude of the love and not of the action which is important. Without love the most spectacular achievements are meaningless – "If I speak in the tongues of men and of angels, but have not love, I am a noisy gong or a clanging cymbal." It is only the shortest of steps from the words of St Paul (I Corinthians 13) to Mother Teresa's request to her Co-Workers to do the "little things", the things no one else has time for, and to do them with great love.

Among the host of activities which could be singled out as examples of small things imbued in this way with great importance, in India the Co-Workers work alongside the Sisters and the Brothers in the most distressing circumstances. Supplies of milk are provided for the children of the slum schools by the efforts of thousands of Danish children

140

and children of the Faroe Islands. Children in England, Ireland and Singapore have saved their pennies to give the slum children a daily slice of bread, and a daily vitamin pill is made possible by the children of Germany. Indian children have provided exercise books, pencils, rubbers, etc. for their less fortunate compatriots and have given of their own time to clean and to play with the occupants of Shishu Bhavan. In Mexico the Co-Workers help the Sisters by giving catechism classes and by teaching children and adults how to read and write. Some go to the homes for sick and abandoned people to clean, wash, cook, mend, administer medicines, give baths, feed the sick or simply to listen to their miseries. In Mauritius a doctor gives his free services once a week to help the poor. In Ethiopia Co-Workers have organised a guaranteed supply of milk to be delivered to the Sisters once a month for the children whose need is all too desperately apparent. In Japan a group of Co-Workers of Okayama go to an institute to fold hundreds and hundreds of swaddling clothes and to make pillowcases for handicapped children, and Singapore Co-Workers help the Red Cross at a Cheshire Home. In Argentina the Co-Workers provide the driver for the boat which carries the Sisters to even the most isolated families. In Ireland a Co-Worker makes with meticulous care a set of stations of the cross to be sent as a gift to Calcutta.

*In Argentina, the Sisters' launch, the "Maria Jose" enables them to visit the poor of the otherwise inaccessible islands.*

It would be impossible to record the full dimensions of this work carried out with immeasurable love for the materially poor of the world and it is in no way to detract from its importance to suggest that the areas of need so far mentioned are largely those with which the affluence of the West and of North America has come automatically and sometimes complacently to associate poverty. Mother Teresa has insisted that writing a cheque from the comfortable vantage point of a cosy, well-furnished living room is not enough and her Co-Workers have responded magnificently by helping with any means available to them in those places where poverty is all too obvious. Yet Mother Teresa has also overthrown all conventional definitions of poverty. The "poorest of the poor" to whose service, like the Missionaries of Charity, the Co-Workers are committed, are not only the hungry, the thirsty, the naked, the homeless, the crippled, the leprosy sufferers and the dying destitutes: they are also the ignorant, the captives, the alcoholics and drug addicts, the bereaved, the unloved, the abandoned, the outcasts and all those who are a burden to human society, who have lost all hope and faith in life. The familiar image of the child with the distended stomach, matchstick limbs and haunted eyes or of the bedraggled occupant of a Dickensian workhouse, often carefully nurtured for the sake of an illusory peace of mind, is not ousted but joined by a host of less readily identifiable and consequently less manageable shapes.

A rather endearing tale recounts how a Sister in London, trying to establish common ground with a lonely old man who had not wanted to let her into his home, told him that like him the Sisters were poor. "Do you wear tights or socks?" he enquired. "Socks", she replied. "Then you are of the poor", was his unquestioning conclusion. To him the criteria for judgement were charmingly simple. To one Co-Worker the definition was so obscure or so obscured that he found himself unable to recognise the poverty which was closest to him. "I have been a Co-Worker for all these years", he confided, "and I have only just realised that the 'poorest of the poor' is my wife". "Today, once more, when Jesus comes amongst his own, his own don't know him!" insists Mother Teresa, "He comes in the rotten bodies of our poor: he comes even in the rich choked by their own riches. He comes in the loneliness of their hearts; and when there is no-one to love them. Jesus comes to you and me and often, very very often, we pass him by." For this reason Mother Teresa has asked Co-Workers in countries where the poverty is initially less striking not to allow their perception of a need which is immediate, unexciting and frequently all too close, to be obscured by the distant image of a poverty which can at times assume a falsely dramatic quality. Diving into poverty, living it and sharing it does not necessarily mean booking a ticket to India or Venezuela for Mother Teresa has called upon those caught up in the materialism of the West to recognise like Ovid that "plenty has made me poor" and she has done so in a way which casts a new and perhaps disturbing light on the familiar words, "the poor are with you always".

Co-Workers have become accustomed to great demands being made upon their energy and resources. A group in India will doubtless remember deciding to organise a children's Christmas party in Calcutta. "How many should we invite and cater for?" they asked. "What about ten thousand?" replied Mother Teresa. Confronted by a row of surprised faces she added as a special concession, "If you can provide the food, the Sisters will provide the children". Ten thousand deprived children experienced their first Christmas party that year. Perhaps most demanding of all, however, is the requirement to identify the need in their own neighbour-hoods, possibly even in their own families and to attempt to lessen that need not merely by providing financial assistance, for money is no cure for loneliness, grief and a sense of being unwanted but by giving from the heart these most precious of all commodities – time, energy, joy and love.

The Co-Workers' "Way of Life" involves a commitment to share in the work of the Missionaries of Charity and this has found a very practical expression in the preparation of buildings used for their mission throughout the world and in the provision of essential furnishings. As, at the invitation of local bishops, the spirit of the Missionaries of Charity began to find outlets in Australia, Europe and North America, the support which had begun in India did not flag. Co-Workers living near one of the centres or prospective centres of the Brothers or Sisters be it in Italy, Belgium or Britain under-took to make of the humble houses which Mother Teresa had selected, or been given, centres suitable for the role they would play in that particular neighbourhood and fit at least for the very simple life of their prospective occupants. It is a tribute to their efforts and enthusiasm that in Belgium the provision of furnishings for a new centre in Ghent was so generous that a long-standing friend of Mother Teresa found herself compelled to remind Co-Workers of the Sisters' strict adherence to their vow of poverty.

In July, 1978 the Sisters started work in Liverpool. In an attempt to alleviate the ever-increasing problem of homeless-ness they opened a home for women who would not other-wise have so much as a roof over their heads. The building made available to them had previously been a Benedictine presbytery, parts of which had not been used for some time. A number of Co-Workers have vivid memories of the amount of restoration and redecorating they carried out after the Missionaries of Charity had moved in before they considered the building really fit for their "little Sisters", and there are still those who spend time before going to their own jobs, combatting the damp on the top floor by stripping back

the walls, sealing them and painting them. So close is the relationship between Co-Workers and the Missionaries of Charity here, that the Sisters laughingly refer to themselves as Mother Sweeney's Sisters, a tribute to the care with which they are looked after by Tom Sweeney, the Chairman of the local Co-Workers, and one from which he derives a self-effacing but obvious joy. So willing and so generous are the Sisters' helpers that during a visit to the home in Liverpool Mother Teresa warned the Co-Workers not to spoil the Sisters. Their poverty must be protected. "For a while", their Superior recalls with undisguised amusement, "they became hesitant to hand over any gifts, and they used to joke about not being able to offer us lifts any more". The gifts upon which the Sisters' work is utterly dependent continue to flow in but there is no real danger of even the humblest offering being taken for granted. One Irishman, hearing that his daughter had been to visit the home was deeply concerned that she should have taken something to help with the work. "I hope you didn't go empty handed", was his instant retort. "No", was his daughter's reply, "I took a cabbage!" "A cabbage, is that all?" came the explosive response. "I did give them an offering as well", the girl protested. The distinct impression remains that the Sisters would have derived as much pleasure from a single cabbage given in this way as from any sum of money.

Across an expanse of vegetable garden from the home for women stands what used to be the parish hall. Here with the help of Co-Workers the Sisters provide a soup kitchen for the tramps and the homeless and lonely men of Liverpool. The fact that local caterers send food four times a week, stall holders in the market are ever generous, left overs from the airport are available if necessary and the home's own vegetable plot is also productive thanks to the labours of the Co-Workers and of the tramps themselves, means that the Sisters cannot only feed their resident women but also provide soup, bread and often cakes for 130 or so tramps each evening. There can be no more powerful endorsement of Mother Teresa's perspective on wealth and poverty than a jumbled procession of misfits from the Welfare State – some of them the jovial epitome of the comic tramp; some of them individuals whose plight might well be dismissed by moral jurors as "self-inflicted"; some of them with homes but alone

*On January 6th, 1971 Mother Teresa received the Pope John XXIII Peace Prize from Pope Paul VI.*

145

and incapable of looking after themselves; one of them an elderly man wearing only a light threadbare jacket who turned to a well dressed helper shivering in the winter cold with the kindly instruction, "You want to put another jumper on, love!" – all of them waiting their turn for a simple meal delivered to them with a love they could find nowhere else.

Close proximity to the work of the Missionaries of Charity cannot fail to emphasise the validity of their message. In a room, loaned to the Missionary Brothers by the Cathedral of St Vibiana the Co-Workers of Los Angeles do their best each week to relieve the work load:

*"Here is collected all that people give us including beds, stoves, furniture, clothing of all kinds, kitchen ware (of which we can never get enough) and carpets which we cut up for those people who have no beds and must sleep on the floor. We work hard sorting and putting items into boxes marked in Spanish, for most of our people are Spanish-speaking. We have racks where all the best clothing is hung and the rest is put in boxes for the people to go through. With a bit of imagination it reminds us of Sak's, Fifth Avenue."*

Amongst all this what is so striking is the gentleness and patience of those who can receive only what others are prepared to give:

*"Some time ago a lady needing large slacks came in. We have difficulty getting large sizes but we did find three pairs and she was so pleased. While she was waiting and looking, another lady came in, and after we had helped the first lady she told us that she, too, was looking for slacks in a large size. As we were searching and not finding any, the first lady turned to the other and said with a smile, 'How stupid of me. I can't wear all these at once', and gave the second lady the best looking pair. They both left happy and we were touched."*

It is this kind of experience which spurs these Co-Workers, working hand in hand with the Brothers, to new service:

*"The Brothers regularly visit the hotels on Skid Row where they know the occupants and their needs. Many are women who have large families and it is difficult for them to get to us. So we load up a car and, piloted by Brother Sam, we go*

*down to different hotels on different days. We lay out our wares on the sidewalk and everyone has a wonderful time. The boxes are soon empty, and we pick them up and return to fill them for another day."*

The joy which radiates from the Missionary Brothers and Sisters of Charity communicates itself to the Co-Workers through combined service; but what of those Co-Workers who carry out their unobtrusive work without the direct inspiration of the Missionaries of Charity and certainly without ever having had personal contact with Mother Teresa herself? What of the woman in Ireland who took a blind, sick Co-Worker into her home for a fortnight's holiday, of the people behind the iron curtain who say mass in secret for the work of Mother Teresa and who circulate literature about her mission with ingenious subterfuge and sometimes at considerable personal risk? What of the countless others in Switzerland and an increasing number of other countries, who have taken it upon themselves to be called out to sit alone at the bedside of a dying stranger, simply in order that that person should feel that there is someone who cares? "This is what I find so remarkable about the Co-Workers today", comments one of the early members of the Marian Society. "We had the advantage of Mother Teresa's personal presence in those early days. She knew us all as individuals, worked alongside us and guided us by her example. Co-Workers of more recent years have captured her spirit without that advantage." Innumerable individuals have undertaken to visit the sick, to sit with the elderly, to take lonely, unwanted people into their homes and to perform other acts of love which, although small, may well call for strength and courage when embarked upon alone; and they have been able to do so because, as Mother Teresa insists, they are members not of an organisation but of a family.

Since her first encounter with the poverty of the West Mother Teresa has constantly stressed the importance of family life, for lack of love in the home can be held responsible for a multitude of social problems. Speaking in a Carmelite Church in Dublin in 1979, she recalled an encounter with a boy with long hair:

"The Sisters go out at night to work, to pick up the people on the streets. They saw a young man there, late at night —

lying in the street and they said, 'you should not be here, you should be with your parents', and he said – 'when I go home my mother does not want me because I have long hair. Every time I went home she pushed me out.' By the time the Sisters came back he had overdosed himself and they had to take him to hospital. I could not help thinking it was quite possible that his mother was busy, with the hunger of our people in India, and there was her own child hungry for her, hungry for love, hungry for her care and she refused it. Bring love into your home. If you really love God begin by loving your child, your husband/your wife. The old people, where are they? They are in some institution, why are they not with you? Where is that crippled child? – in some institution, why is that child not with you? That child, young mothers and fathers, is a gift of God."

To Mother Teresa the home should be a second Nazareth. Family life must take priority even over all other Co-Worker activities. Co-Workers are called upon to make their homes centres of compassion and if necessary to forgive endlessly in the interests of harmony and love, for the love which radiates outwards to embrace innumerable others must begin in the family. Where there are difficulties, the solution to them as to every other "impossible possibility" lies in prayer. "The family that prays together, stays together" is one of Mother Teresa's favourite expressions and if it holds true for families in the generally accepted sense, then it must do so also for what she sees as the extended family of the Co-Workers. Through prayer all differences are harmonised and the isolated are no longer alone but united with others in a strengthening love which paradoxically proclaims that what matters is the individual – a love which makes no moral pronouncements and which calls for no return. Through prayer also, those who seek to love God in their fellow men through wholehearted free service to the poorest of the poor became Co-Workers not of Mother Teresa but of God.

*Make us worthy, Lord, to serve our fellow men throughout the world who live and die in poverty and hunger. Give them, through our hands, this day their daily bread, and by our understanding love, give peace and joy.*

*Lord, make me a channel of thy peace, that where there is hatred, I may bring love; that where there is wrong, I may*

Let us love others as Jesus loves you + me
God bless you
M Teresa

Mother Teresa
Brompton Oratory
Sept. 16th '74

*bring the spirit of forgiveness;*
*that where there is discord, I may bring harmony;*
*that where there is error, I may bring truth;*
*that where there is doubt, I may bring faith;*
*that where there is despair, I may bring hope;*
*that where there are shadows, I may bring light;*
*that where there is sadness, I may bring joy.*

*Lord, grant that I may seek rather to comfort than to be*
*comforted; to understand rather than to be understood; to*
*love rather than be loved; for it is by forgetting self that one*
*finds; it is by forgiving that one is forgiven; it is by dying*
*that one awakens to eternal life. Amen.*

By praying these words daily, Co-Workers throughout
the world are united with the Missionaries of Charity and
with each other. If there is a guarantee against the fiction and

149

diversification which has undermined many a well-intentioned association, it lies in prayer. "Sometimes I find it easy to smile at the poor but not so easy to smile at my fellow Sisters", admits Mother Teresa. The solution lies in the operation not of a personal will influenced by worldly considerations but of a will whose love remains unwavering. For this reason Mother Teresa has repeatedly emphasised the spiritual dimension of the Co-Workers' way of life. Those who speak to schools or other organisations have been asked to concentrate more and more on the development among the Co-Workers of a spirit of love and concern. Activities such as sponsored walks have been transformed into spiritual pilgrimages in order to strengthen the young walkers' understanding of the spiritual nature of the work, committee meetings begin and end with prayer and wherever possible Co-Workers are encouraged to meet regularly at least once a month for an hour of prayer and meditation. In Rome Co-Workers meet in the Chapel of San Gregorio, a group in America gather together in a nursing home, where they are frequently joined by many of the invalid residents, another group assemble in the church hall of a Surrey village where they meditate against the background of their children's chatter, a joyful sound which no-one would dream of stifling. The list of places and countries in which the Co-Workers gather is considerable yet in a common purpose all are mysteriously joined – with each other and sometimes with those they seek to serve – with the colourful band of tramps in Liverpool, for example, who of their own accord come to a Holy Hour, held once a week before the soup kitchen, and join enthusiastically in a rendering of hymns and prayers which is doubtless sometimes unorthodox but all the more spontaneously happy.

Prayer may be silent: "We need to find God, and he cannot be found in noise and restlessness. God is the friend of silence. See how nature – trees, flowers, grass – grow in silence; see the stars, the moon and sun, how they move in silence. Is not our mission to give God to the poor in the slums? Not a dead God, but a living, loving God. The more we receive in silent prayer, the more we can give in our active life; we need silence to be able to touch souls. The essential thing is not what we say, but what God says to us and through us. All our words will be useless unless they come from within

150

– words which do not give the light of Christ, increase the darkness." It is only through prayer that individual action becomes fully effective and is at the same time maintained in its proper perspective.

*Mother Teresa forms the focal point for a gathering of Co-Workers. At her feet sits their International Chairman.*

The International Chairman of the Co-Workers has drawn on a recipe from Mrs Beeton's Household Management as a prime illustration of how love and service should not manifest itself. The recipe is magnanimously entitled "Benevolent Soup", subtitled a "Cheap soup suitable for a soup kitchen" and contains only the very cheapest ingredients. This concept of Victorian benevolence finds its significant reversal in a way of life focused on the words "Make us worthy, Lord to serve our fellow men". The concept of instrumentality, inherent in the prayer of St Francis and constantly reiterated by Mother Teresa, automatically dispels all sense of self-congratulatory benevolence, for only through the loss of self can the individual become an effective channel for a peace, to which all "credit" is due. There can be no question of a loving service which is in fact a largely selfish meeting of some possibly unidentified personal need for a boosting of the ego. Instead the relationship which exists between the Missionaries of Charity or the Co-Workers and the poor is one which entails the surrender of the self in an encounter which is not one of benefactor and humbled recipient but one based on the recognition of the love of God for every individual, for if God loves each person then every meeting with another person involves the unique discovery of that which is the object of God's love in him, of that which comes to him from God. Such a discovery allows no room for condescension or for moral judgement and takes no cognizance of the obsessive search for "concrete results".

The frequency with which a patient presents himself at the door of the Missionaries of Charity, is welcomed, cured and returns to the streets only to reappear at the door a short time later in a similar condition contradicts all Western concepts of a profitable system. Yet Mother Teresa has insisted that her work is with precisely those trapped in a way of life in which self-destruction is almost inevitable, just as she has rejected all attempts to "institutionalise" her mission because it is in the nature of institutions to help those who are most likely to respond to treatment at the expense of those who are labelled incurable. For her there is no incorrigible or incurable person in the usual definition of the words for every situation contains the embryo of a secret promise.

For those prepared to perceive it that promise, she insists, is fulfilled even in the most repellant of hiding places – in the filthy drug addict, the surly, abusive meths drinker, the next door neighbour with the vitriolic tongue, in the baby batterer, or in the stinking vagrant. "There is always something to be learned in the most unlikely places", one Co-Worker beamed and the cliché assumed a new vigour. She had spotted in the corner at one of the Christmas parties given in London for the city's tramps a dejected figure with a particularly repulsive eye infection, whom even his fellow tramps were avoiding. As she approached him, he remarked almost defiantly: "You know, I'm never alone." The Co-Worker looked at him questioningly. "God's always with me", he announced with absolute conviction. This poignant reminder that the Christ who came into this world in the humblest of stables in Bethlehem was the constant companion of this lonely tramp was a source of great joy to her. By no means classifiable as a concrete result, this was nevertheless her "return", spontaneous, unexpected and all-embracing.

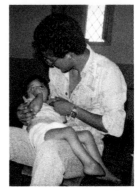

*A Co-Worker is one who chooses a way of life that calls for seeing God in every human being: Co-Workers in Malta tend to the needs of handicapped children.*

Without moral judgements, without the dogged quest for "results" the perception of poverty in all its multifarious forms, so frequently obstructed, becomes clearer. Through the opening of the heart it becomes possible not to seek in another's need the confirmation of a notion already and frequently erroneously conceived but to perceive instead what is really required. An Anglican priest tells the story of two men rushing at the very last moment onto the platform of a railway station. The train was about to leave and the last of the doors were being slammed shut. A would-be helpful passenger opened the door of his compartment, grabbed the first of the flustered arrivals and with a magnificent effort hauled him on board just as the train gathered momentum. The second of the two men was left, bewildered on the platform. For a short interval there was a breathless silence, then the helped man burst into hysterical laughter. Asked why by his confused helper, he replied: "Because", pointing in the direction of his companion abandoned on the platform, "I came to see him off". The intention was the very best but the action was of no constructive use because the perception of the need was imperfect.

Mother Teresa's request to Co-Workers to identify the need which is nearest to them calls for a selfless sensitivity, it demands that kind of perception which recognises when it is that an elderly or invalided person needs to be made to feel useful by being put to work rolling bandages, and when it is that all that is required is a listening and sympathetic ear. A tale with a touch of pathos is told of how, after a group of Co-Workers had been knitting gloves for homeless men for some time, one spokesman from amongst the tramps ventured to ask that the gloves be knitted without ends to the fingers so that, without taking them off, they could more easily pick up cigarette stubs from the streets. The story which speaks eloquently of their plight is also a small but concrete indication of how the full dimensions of need can elude. The openness, the humility and sensitivity called for is possible only when action is a gift of the heart – the fruit of prayer.

"If we don't pray, we don't live, but we are not meant to do only that. The fruit of prayer is love and action is the fruit of love."

Where action, love and prayer are irrevocably linked, the results transcend all definition. So it is that one young girl who works in a geriatric centre insists that where once she saw senility, drooling, shaking, mumbling and incontinency, now she sees only Christ; so it is also that a group of Maltese students working voluntarily in the slums of Sicily experience a joy which outweighs all the difficulty and the sometimes sordid quality of their labours. After one week in Palermo, one of them writes of the "wonderful effects of love".

*"We have instantly formed one community, the Sisters, ourselves and the people, who have accepted us totally. The first week has been a very happy one. We are all content to be here. Some of us are in school, the rest work in the slums. The school consists of singing, learning to read and write, drawing, dancing, etc. But the most important thing is to show the children that you are ready to love them no matter what they do to you. In fact the children are little demons who do not know how to play. Their character is very violent. At the slightest provocation they will turn and say 't'ammazzero', 'I'll kill you'. This is all the fault of the character of the place where the law of the jungle rules. Survival of the fittest. They have to be violent in order to live. We are trying to love them, and to this they have responded with great enthusiasm. They are hungry for love and affection and are very willing to accept once this is offered. They are nearly uncontrollable and very hard headed. They run all over the place breaking, climbing all the windows, fences, and roofs of the convent. One of them smashed a blackboard by charging it with his head! They are very violent with each other and with us. It is a commonplace occurrence for one to hit another with what is near, be it a chair, his shoes or their spoon or fork. We have a running battle with them, pulling, bringing them from the top of a door, etc. We end up by having our clothes torn or as has happened, by being hit with a fork or spoon.*

*"In spite of this the children love us immensely. As soon as they see one of us they run and cling, kiss and hug him. It is a common sight to see each one of us with about four children clinging to him, from his neck, clothes, hair, anything from which they can cling. Most of the boys are dirty and smelly, one reason being that in Palermo water is rationed, ie there is water for only a few hours every day. This is a considerable hardship especially when by the end of the day we ourselves become very dirty and smelly, having been lifting and carrying children smelling of urine on our shoulders and heads all day long. The children have the habit of dirtying our water during the day by putting frogs, soap*

*and other rubbish, or else by immersing their heads in it to cool themselves. They also have sores on account of the dirt of course – some have fleas, bugs and lice for good measure. We sometimes eat the same food as the children, which is very poor indeed. The people like us because they see that we have come to help them, that we are ready to live the same life as they. We have cleared a huge area near the convent and now for the first time the children have a decent football pitch.*

*"The work in the slums has started, and the first impression is that we could never imagine human beings to live in those conditions. I will give you an example. A fifty year old man living in two very small rooms, which were not even fit for pigs. He has no toilet and relieves himself in one of the rooms, he is also blind. He does not seem to care about the way in which he lives."*

Yet, notwithstanding the squalor the writer speaks only of happiness:

*"We are all very happy and very united together, the hardships are nothing compared with the joy of being able to work for our poor brothers. We lack certain material things, but these lose all importance when we are surrounded by all this love and joy."*

Love stands softly at the threshold of a limitless and indeterminable world. Beyond the images so familiar and apparently carefully defined, the rainbow of its merging colours is constantly and vigorously extending.

The habitual search for the security of clear definition must eventually pose the question, "What exactly is a Co-Worker?" Membership of what is emphatically stated not to be an "organisation" in the accepted sense of the word, is dependent only on the desire to "join" and the answers as to what exactly is entailed are many and manifold:

*"A Co-Worker is nothing but the life of Christ shining in the world today.*

*"A Co-Worker is a person who somehow sees a vision similar to that of Mother Teresa and who somehow wants to attempt to live out that vision in daily life. The vision involves seeing God as the benevolent master of all creation and thus seeing him in each and every aspect of creation, especially in the eyes*

*of each and every person encountered. This freeing event releases the Co-Worker from the need to hold on to anything material and correspondingly chains the Co-Worker to the deeply spiritual realities of God and person. The most needful, whether it be spiritual or material, become the special object of the Co-Worker's concern and provides expression for the deep love of God within. A special attachment to the work of Mother Teresa as a 'light in the dark' is expressed both spiritually and materially. In short a Co-Worker is a person who sees the work of Mother Teresa as being and expressing what Christianity really is and who wants to go and be and do likewise."*

*The only cure for the ills of this world of ours, is Love.*

*"A Co-Worker is one who chooses a way of life that calls for*

156

*seeing God in every human being. Seeing God in everyone, starting with those closest to us often calls for a tremendous change, a transformation, and this transformation brings its fruits. We become ready to share ourselves and our possessions with the lonely, the ill, the poor and the unwanted. We learn the immeasurable power of suffering willingly accepted, of forgiveness freely given, and we are strengthened by being part of a world wide company of those who bear witness to the presence of God in every member of the family of man."*

*"A Co-Worker is one who is committed to being a part of God's overall plan for this wonderful world of his, who tries to recognise God's ever present love, in, and through, his fellow men; who is sensitive to the needs of others – ready to love – to share – to step aside and help those who are weak, or those who suffer – ready – if need be, to delay with those who fall by the wayside, understanding that they also, are a part of the glorious whole."*

*"A Co-Worker is one who knows that no tear is ever wasted, that there is no suffering, however terrible, that cannot be shared and ennobled; that in the end, the only meaning – the only cure, for the ills of this world of ours, is Love, because as St John says: 'God is Love'."*

To these definitions of something essentially indefinable must be added Mother Teresa's own thoughts on what it means to be a Co-Worker:

We are using the name of Mother Teresa but we are actually Co-Workers of Jesus.

A Co-Worker is one who loves. People will know us by our love.

It is not so much what we do, but how much love we put into it.

Being a Co-Worker is not doing . . . it is being. It is a calling to *be* with every person we meet.

It is a way of life, not a name. "Love me as I have loved you".

To be a Co-Worker is to belong totally to Jesus.

We must bring more of Jesus, more of the love of Jesus to the people we meet.

We must proclaim Christ by the way we talk, by the way we walk, the way we laugh, by our life, so everyone will know we belong to him.

Proclaiming is not preaching, it is *being*.

We must pray and sacrifice. Our Lord keeps telling us, "Martha, Martha, you must give up many things".

Everyone has something to give.

Holiness is the acceptance of the will of God.

Pray the work. Pray while you work. Offer it up.

Let God use us without consulting us.

Above all, do everything with joy.

Bring prayer back into family life.

We must act so that people can look and see God in us.

What is important is giving freely what has been freely given without taking pleasure in the giving.

Live the life of a Co-Worker and you are a Co-Worker for life. "It is like Baptism."

May the Lord keep you in his heart because it is the only place we can be together.

Asked what being a Co-Worker meant to her personally, one national chairman admitted with some embarrassment that any answer would have to take the form of one of two inappropriate alternatives – either a brief reply which would be hopelessly inadequate or a book devoted entirely to that subject. Reticence to talk of any personal activities carried out in the spirit for which Mother Teresa has said they must strive is a significant and appealing characteristic of the Co-Workers. Most are delighted to talk of the many others whom they know to be doing "marvellous things"; few are prepared to disclose the extent of their own endeavours to live the Co-Workers' Way of Life to the full. It would seem that they have taken to heart Mother Teresa's insistence that proclaiming their Lord does not involve preaching but being with humility of heart. The Co-Workers, she has said, are the branches on the vine of St John's Gospel (John 15:1-17). Tightly joined to the vine, the branches silently, lovingly, unconditionally must allow themselves to be pruned by the Father, for in all life there must be the cross, and then they will bear fruit. It is by this fruit and by the love they bear one another that they are to be identifiable.

The most effective endorsement of the message is not the vain attempt at definition but the medium itself. The Co-Workers themselves must be the most striking witnesses to their own way of love. So it is that a Co-Worker is the nurse in Chicago who has made it her special mission to console dying cancer patients or the owner of a chain of supermarkets in Holland who prepared some 30,000 Christmas gift parcels for the children of Mother Teresa. A Co-Worker is the individual in Madrid who runs a nursery for children whose fathers are in prison or alcoholics so that their mothers can take jobs. Co-Workers are the group in Mauritius who laboured to give a Christmas lunch for one hundred elderly people or those in Australia who provided special mattresses for the home for alcoholic men. A Co-Worker is the occupant of a London prison who sent five pounds for the Missionaries of Charity and promised to pray for them regularly, the woman in Austria who has knitted and sewn innumerable children's clothes, or the one in Brighton who, having helped to make an immeasurable supply of soup and sandwiches over the years, laughingly claimed she did not deserve a mention because she had never made a soufflé.

The list is potentially interminable and all the more so because for every identified, acknowledged act of love there are countless others which remain unidentified, carried out by those small hidden souls whose hearts are true and good and full of love – the souls in whom Brother Andrew recognised a source of all-transcending hope – those who have undertaken quietly and unobtrusively to do the humble things so greatly needed, in the knowledge that giving, if it is to be truly effective, may well hurt.

*In her letter* overleaf *Mother Teresa relates a Papal call for peace to the Co-Workers' Way of Life.*

Missionaries of Charity
54A, Lower Circular Road
CALCUTTA-16.

17/2/79

My dear Co Workers.

The Holy Father in His Speech to the World on the 1st Jan-79 said — No, to Violence

Yes, to Peace —

The 'way of life' of the Co-Workers Seems the most beautiful answer & readiness to answer this call of love — Let us accept this way throughout the world wherever the Co-Workers are or will be — Faith in action is Love & love in action is Service — Therefore 'the way of life' is but the fruit of Faith — Faith has to be put in action of love if it has to live — and love to be true & living — to be God's love in action — must be Service

for us – Miss of Ch. & Your Co Works
the giving of the whole hearted
free service to the Poorest
of the Poor is the living proof
that God loves the world
so much that He keeps
on sending – giving you
& me to be His love in
the world of to day. This is
all Jesus told us – love one
another as I have loved you
as the Father has loved me.
Father's love, Son's love, our love
is but a "giving" until it hurts.
How great is His love for us – He
makes Himself the Bread of life
to satisfy our hunger for love
and then He makes Himself the
hungry one – so that we can
satisfy His love for us. oh, the
Humility of God.
Let us all make 1978

Something beautiful for God
by living — the No to violence with
our tongue and our actions
and Yes to peace with our
tongue & our actions.
I would like & as soon as possi
ble all the co-entrees to use
the "way of life" and avoid
every & any fund raising
means — until such time where
some emergency or need may
happen. then I will ask God
to raise the money — until
then only Sacrifice money. Let
us do this with great love.
The money people give is to
be used only by the MC Poor
the MC Broken & Sisters Serve.
therefore no amounts of money
be kept in different banks
—

Let all money to be sent to Dr M. Coline in London in UK - + other countries to Rome

There is much talla re-organisations useing money given for the Poor - up to now I have never heard about the CoWs let us protect the trust + Love Both the people who give + the Poor for whom it is given let us let us

May the joy of Jesus be your strength to love one another and the bond of unity + peace Let us make 1978 Something beautiful for God by - Saying + living

No to Violence
Yes to Peace

God bless yr
M Teresa M -

# CHAPTER SEVEN

## THE LINK FOR SICK
## AND SUFFERING CO-WORKERS

# Through joy,
# the beauty of the world
# penetrates our soul.
# Through suffering,
# it penetrates our body.

SIMONE WEIL

In August 1948 a Malayalam journalist wrote a moving article entitled "A Sari-dressed European lady", in which he described his impressions of a woman, whom he took at first to be eccentric or peculiar but whom he subsequently recognised as a remarkable person with a mission of overwhelming importance:

*"She has adopted the Indian way of dressing and eating. She wears a sari, takes her food sitting on the floor, doing away with spoons, knives, forks, etc., and sleeps on the floor as cots and such comforts are not meant for one who has devoted her life to the cause of the poor. We know that the Madura Missionary de Nobili lived the life of a Sanyasi and his followers imitated his example for a time. Similarly John de Britte adopted the dress and practices of Hindu Sanyasis. It would appear, however, that this is the first Catholic European lady who has come to render service in India, adopting the Indian mode of dress and customs."*

The article continues:

*"She is ready to render service to anybody who is in need of help whether he or she be a Hindu, Protestant or Catholic.*

164

*The homes of the poor are her special sphere of work."*

It concludes:

*"To understand her courage in undertaking such work, one has only to imagine one of our own women-folk of the same age as she, going alone to render social service among the Negroes of America. There is a great difference between workers like this and those who go to foreign countries and live in communities to do social work . . . People like this are essential to our country."*

Remarkably, the description is not, as might well be expected, of Mother Teresa but rather of Jacqueline de Decker, a young Belgian woman who had come to India with intentions that were strikingly similar to those of Mother Teresa. Some thirty years later she recalls:

*"Since the age of seventeen I had longed to give myself up entirely to God for the poor in India. We were a group of eight lay people who shared the same ideal, but the war separated us. A Jesuit priest asked me to do medical social work in Madras, India; on the day of my departure, on 31st December, 1946, he died unexpectedly but the Bishop of Madras advised me to learn the language and the customs of India. So I worked in a dispensary and gave instructions; for a while I also helped with Ghandi's village work."*

Jacqueline de Decker was a graduate of the great Catholic University of Louvain, where she had specialised in sociology. She had also obtained a Diploma in Nursing and First Aid. After completing her University studies she became a nurse and during the war worked with the British troops, giving invaluable medical assistance in a stricken city, deserted by the vast majority of its doctors. She herself is far too self-effacing, far too conscious that whatever she has been able to do or to give is ultimately attributable to the will of God, to speak of her own acts of courage but there are still many in Antwerp today who remember her commitment to the wounded, the suffering and the helpless. Despite such a prelude, however, Jacqueline de Decker admits to being totally unprepared for the poverty and the sickness of India. Living alone and on a pittance, she won the recognition and the affection of the Indians with whom she worked but she recalls a sense of isolation in the face of so enormous a task:

*"I was advised to seek out Sister Teresa in Calcutta but Sister Teresa was in Patna for a medical training course of three months. There I met her. She was in the chapel, deep in prayer. We talked and discovered that we had the same ideal. We worked together in the hospital in Patna and in Mokanneh but at the end of December, 1948, Sister Teresa returned to Calcutta. In my small address book for India I can still find the entry: 'Sister Teresa, 14 Creek Lane, Calcutta', and all her first letters came from this address."*

Jacqueline de Decker's intention was to join Mother Teresa's order but her time in India had already revealed serious health problems. She would first return to Antwerp for medical attention. In Belgium it was discovered that she was suffering from a severe disease of the spine and that in order to prevent paralysis she would have to undergo a number of operations. Gradually it became apparent that Jacqueline would never be able to return to India and that her total commitment to India's poor and diseased and to what she had so profoundly believed to be God's will for her, was not to be. The initial frustration, the anguish, the sense of having been abandoned by the God in whom she had placed her absolute trust must be passed over. Suffice it to say that there is in her very being an understanding of the spiritual and physical suffering of others, that radiates a sincerity which can only spring from personal experience of transcended doubt and pain. It teaches complete surrender to the often rationally incomprehensible will of God; it proclaims that from every experience, however apparently negative, something positive and spiritually constructive may spring.

For Jacqueline de Decker came the realisation that she was not being rejected by God but being granted instead a special role. Her task was to offer joyfully a life of suffering and pain for the work of Mother Teresa and for the young women who were to become the first Missionaries of Charity. In 1952 she received a letter from Mother Teresa:

*"You have been longing to be a missionary. Why not become spiritually bound to our society which you love so dearly. While we work in the slums you share in the merit, the prayers and the work, with your suffering and prayers. The work here is tremendous and needs workers, it is true, but I*

*need souls like yours to pray and suffer for the work – you'll be in body in Belgium but in soul in India where there are souls longing for Our Lord, but for want of someone to pay the debt for them, they cannot move towards him."*

In Belgium Jacqueline de Decker undertook to pay her part of that "debt" and in India as the Missionaries of Charity increased in number, Mother Teresa's vision of the Sick and Suffering as lives which would form "a burning light consumed for souls" grew accordingly: "I need many people, sick and suffering joining the society as spiritual children", she wrote and then in January, 1953, she drafted the basis for the "Link for Sick and Suffering Co-Workers".

*"I am very happy that you are willing to join the suffering members of the Missionaries of Charity – You see what I mean – You and the others who will join will share in all our prayers, works and whatever we do for souls and you do the same with us with your prayers and sufferings. You see the aim of our society is to satiate the thirst of Jesus on the Cross for love of souls by working for the salvation and sanctification of the poor in the slums. Who could do this better than you and the others who suffer like you. Your suffering and prayers will be the chalice in which we the working members will pour in the love of souls we gather round. Therefore you are just as important and necessary for the fulfilment of our aim. To satiate this thirst we must have a chalice and you and the others – men, women, children – old and young – poor and rich – are all welcome to make the chalice.*

*In reality you can do much more while on your bed of pain than I running on my feet but you and I together can do all things in him who strengthens me.*

*There will be no vows unless some get permission from their confessor to do so. We could get a few prayers we say, for you to say them also, so as to increase the family spirit, but one thing we must have in common – the spirit of our Society. Total surrender to God, loving trust and perfect cheerfulness – by this you will be known as a Missionary of Charity. Everyone and anyone who wishes to become a Missionary of Charity – a carrier of God's love is welcome but I want specially the paralysed, the crippled, the incurables to join for I know they will bring to the feet of Jesus many souls. In our turn – the Sisters will – each one have a Sister who prays, suffers, thinks, unites to her and so on – a second self. You see my dear sister our work is a most difficult one. If you are with us – praying and suffering for us and the work – we shall be able to do great things for love of him – because of you.*

*Personally I feel very happy and a new strength has come in my soul at the thought of you and others joining the society spiritually. Now with you and others doing the work with us, what would we not do, what can't we do for him?"*

*"If you are with us – praying and suffering for us and the work – we shall be able to do great things for love of him."*

In the same letter Mother Teresa listed the names of her first twenty-seven novices. The first ten were to be professed on the 12th April, 1953, and they would be in particular need of a Sick and Suffering link. Recovering from what was only one of the thirty operations which she has undergone to date, Jacqueline de Decker sought among her fellow patients and sufferers for those who would be prepared to pray for an adopted sister, to write to her once or twice a year and, above all, to accept from the heart the mystery of suffering offered in faith and love for the work of a virtual stranger in a far distant land. Mother Teresa's writings to the sick and suffering presented a supreme challenge to faith:

*"How our Lord must love you to give you so much part in His suffering. You are a happy one for you are a chosen one. Be brave and cheerful and offer much for me that I may bring many souls to God. Once you came in touch with souls, the thirst for souls grows daily."*

168

The capacity to see happiness in suffering requires a special kind of vision. To Mother Teresa the call to be a Sick and Suffering Co-Worker is a beautiful vocation. In a letter dated October 1954, she writes:

*What a beautiful vocation is yours - A missionary of Charity - a carrier of God's love. We carry on our body and soul the love of an Infinite thirsty God - and We - you and I, and all our dear Sisters and the S.S. will satiate that burning thirst - you with your untold suffering we with "hard labour", but are we not all the same. - one - " as you Father in me & I in you" said Jesus.*

In the same year, despite the poverty and the rigorous discipline of the order, there were already forty-eight Missionary Sisters of Charity. It goes almost without saying that there were also forty-eight Sick and Suffering ready to share in the spirit of the society and to offer their pains for a "second self".

The apparent meaninglessness and horror of suffering has always represented one of the principal stumbling blocks to belief in a God of love and life. Confronted by his own pain or by the evident suffering of another, man so frequently cries out that no loving and omnipotent deity could permit such horrors and the answer that they are the product, not of God's love but of man's sin seems all too frequently unsatisfactory or incomplete. To the Christian, the world of wretchedness may well be the world in which there is no faith in God. In Romans 1:29-31, St Paul depicts with vivid eloquence man in the mire of the Roman Empire of his day:

*"They were filled with all manner of wickedness, evil, covetousness, malice. Full of envy, murder, strife, deceit, malignity, they are gossips, slanderers, haters of God, insolent, haughty, boastful, inventors of evil, disobedient to parents, foolish, faithless, heartless, ruthless."*

This vivid condemnatory vocabulary was not, however, applicable only to the Empire for Jew, Greek, Gentile alike – all were in need of salvation. Paul was here describing the state that was subsequently to be termed "original sin" and to him the means of salvation from such wretchedness was faith. Man is liberated or "justified" by faith and the recurring theme of Romans is that "he who through faith is righteous shall live" (Romans 1:17). Given the presence of faith in man, the onus would appear to be thrown back on to God to give life or to "heal". Yet how many of the "faithful", how many truly remarkable people whose faith in God has withstood countless trials are still confined to wheelchairs or prostrated on beds of pain? If the solution to suffering lay in the simple exchange of faith for physical health, doubtless the number of sick would be drastically reduced. Instead, the problem of suffering appears to many like an all too poignant confirmation of 1. Corinthians 1:19, "I will destroy the wisdom of the wise and the cleverness of the clever I will thwart", for it is significant that while so many of the great religions claim to heal, this healing process is often paradoxical, to such an extent that death cures and sickness strengthens. In this paradox lies all the mystery of a faith which enables Mother Teresa to urge her Sick and Suffering to see their pains as a "beautiful vocation". This is an advocation of complete surrender to the will of God. It is not indifference to their agony but at the same time it does not teach a desperate clinging to an ideal of physical health and comfort for it is based on the recognition that suffering calls for even greater faith and love, and that faith in God's love and the saving death of his Son is the path to salvation or indeed to true "healing".

This kind of healing is not necessarily the restoration of some stereotype of normality or social adaptability – it does not necessarily consist of the patching up of wounds or the mending of broken bodies and torn flesh. True healing, it may be suggested, is more positive and more durable – it is progress and resurrection and it is best understood in the contemplation of the wounds of the risen Christ which did not disappear altogether but which were instead glorified, transformed and somehow beautiful:

*"Put your finger here, and see my hands; and put out your hand, and place it in my side." (John 20:27)*

There is nothing romantic, poetic or obviously beautiful about the illnesses listed beside the names on the records of the Sick and Suffering: Parkinson's disease, crippling arthritis, osteomalacia in the foot causing pain and lameness, cancer, multiple sclerosis, spinal defects causing constant pain, polio, angina, severe blood disorder, leaking heart valve, mentally sick, blind or simply "chronically ill". The long list of diseases, many of them incurable, conjures up a heart-rending vision of stricken men and women of all ages, wrestling all too understandably not only with their own physical pain but also with a sense of bitterness, despair and disillusionment with a manifestly uncompassionate God. Yet nothing could be further from the truth. Those sick people who come into contact with the work of Mother Teresa and who express an interest in it are sent an outline of Mother Teresa's concept of the link with the Sick and Suffering with an explanation and frequently a warning that replies to letters to their linked Brother or Sister may well be few and far between. The following notes provided as "Guidelines for the Links for the Sick and Suffering" give a brief idea of how the system works:

*"The sick and those unable to join in activities may become a close Co-Worker of an individual Sister or Brother by offering their prayers and suffering for such Sister or Brother" (Constitution of the International Association of Co-Workers of Mother Teresa).*

*1) Anyone who, by reason of age, handicap or suffering is unable to undertake works of charity is welcome to become a Co-Worker Member of the Link for the Sick and Suffering.*

*2) He/She should apply to the Local Branch of the Co-Workers and will receive the prayer and Co-Workers Way of Life, the leaflets and newsletters.*

*3) The National Co-ordinator will send the name and full address of the applicant to the International Link with the Sick and Suffering, Mlle. Jacqueline de Decker.*

*4) The International Link will send the name and full address of a Brother and Sister of the Missionaries of Charity with whom the applicant is to be linked and to whom he or she can write. Applicants should not expect constant correspondence from such Brother or Sister, but should always keep them in their prayers and should try themselves to live in the spirit of the Missionaries of Charity. This means:*

*Joy     Confidence     Poverty*

*5) The names of the sick and suffering will be added to the National Card Index of Co-Workers in order to send them the Newsletters regularly. It is suggested that the Local Branch should visit Co-Worker Members of the Link for the Sick and Suffering or invite them to their meetings.*

Beyond these somewhat impersonal "Guidelines" lies a wealth of love and understanding to which remarkably many, whose lives would perhaps otherwise appear, at least to them, without purpose, find themselves able to respond. The letters of Sick and Suffering Co-Workers to the Sisters or Brothers with whom they are linked or to the national or international co-ordinators frequently betray an instant and almost intuitive understanding of that beautiful but mysterious vocation to which Mother Teresa has said they are called:

*"Dear Sister . . ."*

writes one woman who has been confined to her bed for many years . . . *"How happy I was yesterday to receive your name, to become your co-worker. Truly what a grace it is for me. With all my heart I shall be with you in spirit and in my prayers and I thank you for accepting me. The idea of my being able to do something for a missionary – I who have never been able to travel anywhere – has brought great serenity."*

Another echoes her sentiments almost exactly:

*"Thank you from the bottom of my heart for your beautiful letter which brought me: 'serenity'. To be able to do apostolic work from the depths of my confinement is a real comfort and I promise to apply myself to it faithfully."*

To suggest that there are those who are able to accept the role of "living with Jesus on the cross every day" so readily is not to lose sight of the pain and the heartbreak. One sufferer from polio describes her own difficulties in adjusting from a relatively active life to that of a helpless invalid:

*"You see, when one becomes disabled, 'struck down' as some people like to say, especially if one has lead a pretty active life, then one is beset by the 'do gooders', the holy hens*

*"Suffering in itself is nothing but suffering shared with Christ's passion is a wonderful gift."*

172

*to 'accept' or 'offer up' this truly awful, unreal event in one's life . . . The first six months were hell, in a room with five others, who were much older than me and who had been there for many years. One was almost told when one should breathe. Around came all those 'holy hens' wth their 'offering up' and their 'accepting'. I couldn't of course, no-one can ever see the light at the end of the tunnel for about six months. Then gradually, dimly one saw some sort of pattern."*

*Mlle Jacqueline de Decker ventures into the snow of Oslo, in the company of the very first Sisters to join the Order of the Missionaries of Charity – Sister Agnes and Sister Gertrude.*

The following letter from a French woman to Jacqueline de Decker, asking to be considered as a member of the Link for the Sick and Suffering, provides an even more poignant insight into the anguish which accompanied her illness:

*"It is eighteen months since I heard the appeal of Mother Teresa to the sick and handicapped, asking them to join with her and her sisters, by the offering of their suffering and their prayers and for eighteen months I have been unable to forget it. What an open window for one who is shut in physically and mentally by these four walls. I have a great deal of admiration for Mother Teresa and her work and I would be so happy to be associated with it but I do not feel myself worthy. My spiritual life is so poor – I have difficulty in praying, difficulty in focusing my attention, the anguish is ever ready to reappear – what can I offer while I am so weak? In a few words, here is my life – for three and a half years I*

*have suffered from acute respiratory problems. I underwent a tracheotomy and for eighteen months now I have lived with intermittent respiratory assistance. I am linked up to a machine for the night and for part of the day – a greater or smaller part according to the time of the year (In summer, for example, I have needed assistance for the full twenty-four hours; in winter I have been known to cut it down to ten hours). The rest of the time I am on oxygen. I can still move about but only very little and with great difficulty – very rarely outside my room. The cause – Tuberculosis which I contracted as an adolescent and for which I spent twelve consecutive years in sanatoriums. I was left with the after-effects and when I reached forty there were problems which necessitated the tracheotomy, etc.*

*I am forty-five years old, single, a secretary by profession. Having arrived at the end of my life, I am frightened by the flatness and the emptiness of it. I shall come before God with empty hands. For nearly thirty years I turned my back on him. I did not want to 'lose' my life but to possess one of my own! Sad folly. I was so aware of the fact that a few years ago I asked God to do anything, it didn't matter what, to extract me from the mud – I would accept illness if necessary. Shortly afterwards I fell ill. I think that the answer to my prayer exceeded my expectations. A labourer at so late an hour, could I still work in the vineyard of the Father? Am I dreaming, to think that I could become part of the beautiful chain of love that Mother Teresa is proposing? I place myself in your hands – those of a friend who does not know me – but you must know how weak I am and how I fear suffering and avoid it whenever possible and how I must struggle sometimes to combat the feeling of panic. I would make a very feeble Co-Worker but I am confident that the Lord will support me if that is his will.*

*Thank you for the kindness you have shown in reading this. Whatever your answer may be, I shall remain in my heart and in my prayers, close to Mother Teresa, her Sisters and Brothers, and her Co-workers."*

The essence of Jacqueline de Decker's reply may be inferred from this second letter:

*"Your letter which was so warm overwhelmed me with joy . . . I shall try to follow your advice – to place all my*

*trust in Jesus and no longer to cling like a drowning man, but how difficult it is to recapture the soul of a child – to let things be, to cease to fear because it is he who guides our footsteps – to make myself flexible when I am inclined to become rigid. I shall try and with the grace of God I must succeed. I must if I am to become a useful little servant. There is no time to lose."*

Shortly after receiving with great joy the name of the Sister with whom she was to be linked, the writer died.

At its most fundamental, the giving of a sense of purpose to those whose pain-wracked or anxiety ridden existence is apparently without meaning is a wonderful gift. It means, for example, that the husband of a sick Italian woman can write the following:

*"I must thank you for having linked my wife with one of Mother Teresa's Sisters.*
*My wife, who as you know, has been suffering periodically since 1968 with nervous depression, had to undergo an operation for which she felt totally unprepared. She wrote to her Sister and offered all her suffering for her. They write to each other regularly now and my wife has begun to understand that there is a profound reason for her moral suffering, her personal solitude and her anguish. She is better able to accept the fact of being deaf and in pain. She used to say repeatedly that she was no good for anything, that it would be better for her to die. Believe me a transformation has taken place in her. She is still suffering, possibly even more than before, but she knows that she is suffering for a little sister who has need of her suffering and her prayers."*

Yet this kind of "transformation", the serenity of which so many of these people speak, points softly beyond so ego-centred a principle as the need for a personal sense of purpose to something much greater and much more profound. Just as the great mystery of the joy which characterises the Missionaries of Charity lies in the fact that it is still possible in situations of misery and human suffering which in themselves should engender sadness and despair, so what is so striking about the letters of the Sick and Suffering is the courage and the joy which reverberates from between the lines.

*"Yes, I am in great pain" writes an invalid, "but nothing must be lost of this treasure. When I have no more strength I simply offer everything for my little M.C. sister. When my back hurts and my shoulder and my knees seem to be knotted together, giving me pain with every movement and preventing me from falling asleep, then I begin to travel in my thoughts with my little sister from India and with my seminarian from Africa, and in the Carmel of Madagascar I remain in silence, worshipping the Lord before the monstrance which I donated. And the fatigue of so long a journey at last brings me sleep, and I am happy to fall asleep after a night of mission work of this kind."*

Such happiness, it may be suggested, is evidence of a healing process, but it is a healing effective not at the level of the physical but at the level of that existential anguish or anguish of the soul which many have seen as the natural state of man without faith in God. This healing stems from the recognition of the significance of the wounds shown to Thomas and from acceptance in faith, for the risen Christ can only be grasped by love in an act that is beyond concepts, images and rational thought. Many of the Sick and Suffering Co-Workers bear striking witness to the intellectually incomprehensible paradox inherent in the fact that healing of the intangible part of man may well result from affliction of the body. The words of a man suffering from diabetes and a stroke causing almost total blindness reiterate the writings of St Paul:

*"I am now almost completely blind so please tell the Brother that I cannot write to him but of course I can pray. People seem to think that because you are ill you should reject God but I found that through sickness and suffering I have grown to know him better and feel that he wants me to use my illness to help others."*

They express quite spontaneously the same recognition that suffering has not alienated him from but rather drawn him closer to God and convey the same sense of constructive instrumentality in the hands of his maker (2 Corinthians 12: 7-9).

*"And to keep me from being too elated by the abundance of revelations, a thorn was given me in the flesh, a messenger of*

177

*Satan to harass me, to keep me from being too elated. Three times I besought the Lord about this that it should leave me; but he said to me, 'My grace is sufficient for you, for my power is made perfect in weakness'. I will all the more gladly boast of my weaknesses, that the power of Christ may rest upon me."*

This indefinable illness of St Paul's is presented as a means of inducing that kind of weakness which makes him a more effective channel for the power of God. Suffering seen in this light becomes almost a mark of the special presence of Christ, a presence which can find its expression in a fresh vision of the universe in which the demons no longer induce panic and the sirens no longer seduce:

In a clean but shabby flat at the very heart of a great Western city a young man lies motionless on a low bed in the corner of a dimly lit room. For eight of his thirty years he has been paralysed from the neck downwards. Prior to his accident he was a student of medicine with every promise of a brilliant future; now he is dependent for his every move on the help of his old age pensioner mother. He can hear and he can speak but his eyesight is gradually failing.

*"At first", he admits, "I was very bitter, particularly because the medical profession to which I had wanted to devote my life seemed so ineffectual when it came to actually doing something to help me. I couldn't accept the indignity, the helplessness of it all, and 'acceptance' is undoubtedly the key word."*

*"Then", he laughs delightedly, "I came to realise that even this kind of state has its own peculiar dignity, that it was only really my own bitterness that was undignified. When your body lets you down, you are thrown in on yourself, you discover new resources and the phenomenal world appears in a new and totally different light. Believe it or not, between these four rather dingy walls, flat on my back, studying every tiny crack in the ceiling, I have discovered exactly what William Blake meant when he described what it was:*

> *'To see a world in a grain of sand*
> *And heaven in a wild flower,*
> *Hold infinity in the palm of your hand*
> *And eternity in an hour'."*

*"I'll quote you some more poetry", he smiles and the eyes, which can now only just make out the cracks in the ceiling, carry their own distinctive light.*

> *"Truth is within ourselves, it takes no rise*
> *From outward things, whate'er you may believe*
> *There is an inmost centre in us all*
> *Where truth abides in fullness; and around*
> *Wall upon wall, the gross flesh hems it in*
> *This perfect clear perception – which is truth."*
>
> Robert Browning

*"It's true, you know and it would help so many people if only they would realise it."*

Almost unconsciously and very beautifully, this extraordinarily contented young man was echoing the common voice of the mysticism of so many faiths:

> *"Hold fast to thy centre and all things shall be thine",*
> *"Take your seat within the heart of the*
> *thousand-petalled lotus",*
> *"The Kingdom of Heaven is within you."*

For the Christian an essential part of the discovery of the Kingdom of Heaven within, lies in the endeavour to identify with Christ, the perfect man who died to save others. To serve mankind for Christ, is to die with him that they may live. To become a channel of God's love is thus not merely to be a recipient of that love but to be a means of conveying it to others not necessarily through an act of conscious personal will but rather by accepting and allowing the operation of the power of God not so much through the head as through the heart centre – hence "the power which is made perfect in weakness". That the sick who might themselves justifiably make constant demands upon any resources of love should repeatedly express concern for the welfare of others and a desire to help in any way possible, is at the very least impressive. Writing of the Missionaries of Charity, a sufferer from multiple sclerosis makes light of her own pains:

*"Don't they do wonderful work. It makes my aches and pains seem very little when I think of the work those good nuns do."*

Such sentiments are repeated time and time again. The

love given quite literally "until it hurts" is unlimited:

*"Sister M says that my prayers and suffering have helped her, bless her. She will never realise just what joy it gives me to pray and suffer for one who is doing such great work for God. She calls me her 'Mother in Christ' so you see, she is not just my linked Sister, but my very dear daughter in Christ, as well."*

With touching humility those whose strength is already heavily taxed offer the residue to help others:

*"I like to think that, though I haven't much strength, when Sister is hauling on her net, I am just pulling with her, even if it is rather feebly."*

For those prepared to accept, such an offering is in itself an intimation of the divine. Others must inevitably seek proof of its efficacy.

In February, 1973 Mother Teresa gave an address on the care of the destitute at the Sidney Myer Music Bowl, Melbourne:

*"Here in Melbourne," she told an enraptured audience, "we have a home of compassion. We have people who have no one, who roam the streets, for whom maybe only gaol and the road are the only places. And one of them was very badly hurt by another friend of his, another companion. Thinking that the matter was very serious, somebody asked him, 'Who did that to you?' And the man started telling lies, but he wouldn't give the name. And after the person had gone away, I asked him, 'Why did you not tell who hurt you?' And the man looked at me and said, 'his suffering is not going to lessen my suffering'."*

*"This", said Mother Teresa, "is 'Love one another as I have loved you'."*

The attitude of this destitute man that "his suffering is not going to lessen my suffering", Christ-like as it is as an expression of love involving an element of self-sacrifice, is nevertheless readily comprehensible in purely human, rational terms. It has as its basis the familiar schoolboy commandment "Thou shalt not tell tales". The principle that "my suffering can lessen his" is infinitely more difficult to understand, yet the two are not so very far removed from each other. To Mother Teresa the common denominator proclaims itself to the world in the simple but all important direction of her Lord: "Love one another as I have loved you". To her there can be no doubt as to the efficacy of such a love. Her own carefully cherished relationship with Jacqueline de Decker includes an absolute conviction that her capacity to do God's work among the poorest of the poor is closely dependent upon the offering up of the Belgian woman's pains — so much so that when Mother Teresa feels a renewal of energy in herself she is able to predict with uncanny accuracy that the sufferings of her second self will be intensified. This relationship is a source of strength and a fountain of great joy to Mother Teresa. In a later letter addressed to "My dear Jacqueline and all my other children" she writes with compassion but gladness:

*"The weather is very hot – but we gladly offer all this with you for souls – I am very sorry to hear that so many of you are so ill but I am also very glad because I know you are loving God more through all this suffering and are helping us to bring souls to God."*

In her rejoicing she is by no means alone, as the following letter from a Missionary Sister of Charity in Madurai to her Sick and Suffering Co-Worker demonstrates:

*"I received your kind and humble letter and I appreciate your kind and generous offer. Sacrifices and prayers are far more important than all my preaching. You will surely be of great help for our Apostolate in Madurai. We can work together and save souls together for our Lord. The Madurai Mission is yours.*
*The harvest is very great here. Surely you are not a hidden link in a chain but a great help in the Garden of the Lord. The hard work of the gardener alone is not enough for the plants to grow. It also needs sun, wind and rain and my preaching and work is the work of the gardener. So I am very happy to have you as my partner. We will join together and reap a rich harvest for our heavenly Gardener so please pray for me and all my Sisters and poor people in Madurai."*

Another Sister confides in her Sick and Suffering link:

*"The offering of your suffering and your love for me, to Jesus and Mary, has given me so much strength and courage*

*during the past year, to give myself to him totally, through the vows of poverty, chastity and obedience and of service to Jesus in the poor. I thank you for it and I also offer myself, my work and my sacrifices for you. Although I am far from you, you are with me in thought and in the life of love."*

The offerings of those whom Mother Teresa is convinced "can do most" would appear to have borne fruit.

There are in the world today approximately 2,000 Sick and Suffering Co-Workers who have accepted the demanding and paradoxical call to "love and serve Jesus not for what he gives but for what he takes" and who have responded to the direction to "smile at Jesus" which recurs like a leitmotiv throughout Mother Teresa's letters. From a multitude of lands including:

| | | | |
|---|---|---|---|
| England | Ireland | USA | Luxembourg |
| Mauritius | Malta | Canada | Switzerland |
| Spain | S Africa | Venezuela | Japan |
| Singapore | India | Germany | Haiti |
| Austria | Italy | Denmark | Brazil |
| France | Belgium | | |

Also several iron-curtain countries

they offer themselves in the conviction that they are united in the deepest mystery of faith with Jesus on his cross. Young and old, men and women, from all walks of life and afflicted with every conceivable illness and handicap, they form a spiritual link in Mother Teresa's "chain of love around the world" and, frequently from the opposite corner of that world, the Missionary Sisters and Brothers of Charity respond.

The system is not perfect. The rapidity with which the Sisters and Brothers can be moved from one country to the next inevitably gives rise to problems in locating them. For this reason and because of unreliable postage systems the letters which may well represent an invaluable part of this spiritual relationship can go astray. Misunderstandings can arise. Sick and Suffering Co-Workers may not at first fully appreciate that the link must remain an essentially spiritual one, personal gifts and donations to individual Sisters are not permitted; they may feel discouraged by the infrequency of replies from Missionaries of Charity who are only allowed to write to them twice a year and who sometimes do not even fulfil this small quota. For their part, the Sisters and Brothers, caught up in the immediacy of the need which surrounds them, may not always appreciate how much a letter from them would mean to their Sick and Suffering link. Yet miraculously, these difficulties are for the most part overcome. The national co-ordinators struggle nobly to keep in touch with their Sick and Suffering, and submerged beneath countless files and mountains of correspondence, in Antwerp, Jacqueline de Decker compiles innumerable letters, each one written by hand because the use of a typewriter causes a pain which is now intolerable. In this way she remains remarkably up to date with the movements of the Missionaries of Charity and herself keeps in touch with those, whose pains she can in the fullest sense appreciate. She and others are also able to provide a solution to language difficulties by translating with meticulous care the letters of many whose English is weak.

*At the Mother house in Lower Circular Road the Sisters squat or kneel on the bare floor for the Adoration of the Sacrament.*

Where there is a need on the part of the Sick and Suffering Co-Worker, ideally healthy Co-Workers are ready and available to meet it; where the Sick and Suffering are disheartened, they are offered reassurance. Those who are despondent at the absence of response from their link are gently reminded that it is they who are the spiritually mature links in the chain, and not the young Sister or Brother who may well be unready as yet to appreciate fully the nature and importance of such a relationship.

"Pope John XXIII, speaking on suffering stressed the need to find a purpose in it. 'In the love of Christ there is no life without suffering.' So," writes one of the Brothers, "we cannot escape it and we must do all we can to help one another find a purpose in it. If one can find a purpose for suffering by accepting his cross as Jesus Christ accepted His then one will never feel alone."

At its most fundamental the link for the Sick and Suffering has fulfilled this function, but over and above even this, many of its individual members may be seen as living witnesses to Mother Teresa's claim that holiness is not the privilege of the few.

*"Holiness,"* she says, *"does not belong to a small group, however much it may be a luxury to be called holy. It is a simple duty for each one. To this end God made us. Jesus said 'Be ye perfect even as my father is holy.' That is all we have to do – the road to holiness is love – love each other as God loves each one of us. Love until it hurts!"*

In a letter, welcoming a new member of the Sick and Suffering, one national co-ordinator, herself no stranger to suffering, summarises rather beautifully the whole concept:

*"This concept that one person can offer their prayers and sufferings to aid another to carry out God's work with greater love is not one that everybody understands but those who listen to the Holy Spirit within them, know that they are being asked to be channels of his power and love. You who have suffered so much already yet speak with gratitude to God for the 'pain which is life' are clearly one of those chosen for this special vocation. Somewhere I read – was it something of Teilhard de Chardin? – a description of the world as God might see it, a world encompassed with dark clouds of sin and strife but penetrating the gloom are a multitude of brilliant lights, each one a soul at prayer, reflecting God's love, and this is the power that moves the world forward according to his plan."*

# CHAPTER EIGHT

## THE CONTEMPLATIVE LINKS

# "Had he not withdrawn so far into solitude with God, Christ would never have advanced so far into the society of man."

URS VON BALTHASAR

Somewhere beyond the records and the figures which provide concrete and indisputably convincing evidence of a growth of action, the presence and the efficacy of a kind of power house of prayer playing out its less tangible but no less effective role in the development of a universal mission makes itself softly but persistently apparent. Mother Teresa, for whom this power house is doubtless no less real and infinitely more powerful than any of the more concrete sources of energy, has taken every possible opportunity of tapping its limitless resources. The greater the call for action, the greater the call for prayer for the two factors cannot be disassociated from each other. It appears to have been with this kind of principle in mind that in 1976 on the feast of the Sacred Heart, Mother Teresa established a second group of Sisters in New York, a new Contemplative branch of the Missionaries of Charity now known as the Sisters of the Word. The particular mission of these Sisters is to live the Word of God in Eucharistic Adoration and Contemplation and to proclaim the Word to the people of God by their presence and spiritual works of mercy in order that "the Word made flesh will remain in the hearts of men". The new branch provided a role for those whose vocation was to the contemplative life, in a pattern of prayer which nevertheless included several hours in the afternoons for active apostolic work amongst the poorest of the poor. From New York the Sister in charge writes of their work:

*"Our house is in the Bronx area of New York. People are frightened to come where we are and yet the Lord has chosen this place for us and it is the right place, as here we have the most needy – people with a broken spirit. We are surrounded by burnt homes. A drunkard comes in and asks for a rosary. The same fellow comes back with a little bouquet of flowers for the tabernacle. Children ring the bell: 'We want to see Jesus', they say, 'I want to pray with God'."*

Soon after the Contemplative Sisters were founded, Mother Teresa established a similar contemplative branch for men. From their house in Rome, a Missionary Brother of the Word writes of "an everyday life which is more than can be described on a sheet of paper":

*"Two to three hours are spent for apostolic work among the spiritually poorest of the poor in the house or outside by our prayer, presence and sharing. Following the example of Jesus Christ the Good Shepherd, we go out to seek the lost sheep to proclaim the Good News:*

*— to the alcoholics and drug addicts on the streets or wherever they are found.*
*— to the abandoned sick people in the hospitals, or houses or anywhere.*
*— to the lonely and the aged.*
*— to the prisoners – even though in the eyes of the world they are criminals, in the eyes of God they would be guilty – to encourage them to seek mercy and forgiveness from God.*
*— to pray with the men at Carlo Cattaneo – a night shelter run by the Sisters of the Missionaries of Charity of Mother Teresa, for the homeless and abandoned in and around the central railway station in Rome – to celebrate the Sacrament of Reconciliation and the weekly adoration with them.*
*— to encourage the down-hearted, to give sight to the spiritually blind by praying with and for them, accepting them unconditionally as our Heavenly Father accepts us.*
*— to comfort them in sorrow, to befriend them in their*

*loneliness, to sustain them in time of temptation and counsel them when they are in doubt. In a word, to be available to anyone who is most in need of spiritual help and material help, if and when absolutely necessary and there is no one else to help them."*

*In 1974 Father Georges Gorrée, the Chairman of the French Co-Workers became the link between the enclosed Orders and the centres of the Missionaries of Charity with whom they were "twinned".*

The two to three hours so spent are the accompaniment and the product of a routine of deep prayer.

In September 1974 Mother Teresa expressed the wish to see each of her congregation's houses "spiritually adopted" by one or more contemplative communities of other orders throughout the world. Her hope was that these contemplative communities and enclosed orders would by their prayers and their life of silence and renunciation uphold the Missionaries of Charity in their life of active service among the poorest of the poor. At her request, a French priest and Chairman of the French Co-Workers undertook the promotion of such a link and within a year approximately four hundred convents had accepted with great enthusiasm the concept of a spiritual "twinning" which entailed the special remembrance of their adopted convent of the Missionaries of Charity during their usual daily prayers and work. For those older orders where vocations were in short supply, the prospect of a concrete link with a young and vital Congregation for which there was no shortage of applicants and in which there was no lack of vigour, frequently meant a welcome injection of life and a renewed sense of purpose. One male Co-Worker remembers with a great sense of privilege being awarded the singular honour of an invitation to enter beyond the otherwise forbidding walls of an enclosed order of nuns to speak of Mother Teresa's work. The warmth with which the news was received left an indelible impression on his memory.

"All those of us who are called to the contemplative life find ourselves at the heart of the Church and the heart of the world and our mission is to keep this contemplative dimension alive in the Church. Urs von Balthasar has written, 'Had he not withdrawn so far into solitude with God, Christ would never have advanced so far into the society of man' – so that our Missionary of Charity Sisters can go forward with Christ as far as possible into the society of man, let us be willing to withdraw with him as far as we are able into solitude with God." This response from one Mother Abbess was characteristic of many. There are now some 440 Contemplative monasteries in France, Spain, Germany, Belgium, Italy, Canada, England, Luxembourg and other countries, who are committed to upholding the Missionaries of Charity in a way which must remain something of a mystery but one which has the undoubted recognition and appreciation of the Missionaries of Charity themselves and one for which modern science is now compelled to recognise a scientifically identifiable foundation. "If each day I can manage to devote myself to the lepers", claims one Sister in Calcutta, "it will be because far away, in Canada, contemplative Sisters are praying for us", and science has now shown that an exchange of energies of the kind suggested is by no means impossible, or at least that a link of this kind is a "possible impossibility".

Research into the field of consciousness has shown that the brain emits faint electrical impulses which vary in relation to the varying states of consciousness and which can be measured in microvolts by an electroencephalograph. Extensive experiments with individuals engaged in various forms of meditation and contemplation have revealed that the level of consciousness achieved in this kind of activity, which has been described as a level of "relaxed awareness with a move towards interiority", is consistently associated with what are known as Alpha brainwaves. "High amplitude Alpha" indicates that the subject is in a rather deep state of concentration connected with more advanced meditation and with mysticism. Associated with this rhythm is the process in which the individual goes beyond discursive reasoning and yet remains alert and aware in a state of consciousness where the mind does not go out to an object in order to analyse it rationally but rather takes in the whole to "contemplate" or gaze upon it. Associated with this rhythm also is the release of what scientists have called "passive energy". It has been recognised that intuitive, non-rational "thinking" found pre-eminently although not exclusively in religious meditation and contemplation, can produce a recordable energy which is controllable by "passive volition". William Johnston in his study of mysticism in the perspective of both traditional religious insight and modern scientific discovery, "Silent Music", draws on the directions of the Bhagavad Gita for an example of "passive volition": "The Bhagavad Gita tells us to work without coveting the fruits of our labour. In other words, we want the fruit but we don't want it at all, and we are wholly detached. In Zen one's aim is 'satori'. Yet one does not strive or strain for this experience; and if one does, one will not get it." Striving becomes in some way a passive state so that in Christian contemplation the love of God induces a cessation of discursive activity and a consequent release of passive energy.

An excursion into the world of science, even one as brief as this, can provide those inclined to question with "evidence" which reaches ever further into areas previously considered to belong strictly to the "unscientific" and throw an interesting light upon the whole concept of "spiritual linking". William Johnston stresses the importance of the discovery of passive energy precisely because "it demonstrates to the scientist that the Carmelite monastery, the Carthusian hermitage, the Hindu ashram and the Zen temple are not a refuge for people who want to waste time. They are generating large quantities of a very high and precious energy". Ultimately, however, there is the inevitable confrontation with the wounds shown to Thomas – the requirement for a step in the dark. Whether this energy can be seen as the material basis for a higher, unlimited, spiritual energy of the kind which some have claimed builds the earth, and others have seen as the substance of miracles remains a matter for subjective opinion determined by something which itself cannot be confined to the realms of discursive activity – namely faith.

The combined picture of the contemplative links, the Sisters and Brothers of the Word, the Missionaries of Charity and the Co-Workers emerges as one of vital and vibrant interaction and interdependence operative at both the physical and the spiritual level. Speaking of the relationship between the Missionaries of Charity and the Co-Workers, their international chairman refers to the wounds of Jesus: "Mother Teresa once said to me: 'We now have the five wounds of Jesus – the wound in the

> Right Hand – The Contemplative Sisters
> Left Hand – The Contemplative Brothers
> Right Foot – The M.C. Sisters
> Left Foot – The M.C. Brothers
> The Heart – The Co-Workers'.

Don't you think that we can all take shelter in his Sacred Wounds? The Contemplatives are the Hands because they join in prayer. The Feet are the Active Missionaries of Charity because they are all over the world. The Heart is the Co-Workers, because the heart of the world is the home, and that is where the Co-Workers are. We can all take shelter in his Heart." In the prayer upon which the action is seen as dependent it becomes possible to recognise a silent music capable, if given the opportunity, of absorbing the discordant voices of humanity in a mysterious harmony. The imagery is infinitely variable and more or less meaningful according to individual taste and conviction; what must stand as the final recommendation of this corporate mission to the world at large is the fact that it has worked, and it has done so despite the fact that it is made up of individuals susceptible to every human frailty. Among its members are a striking number of "hidden, unknown, saints" but not all those committed to this service of love are spontaneously spiritual giants. The Missionaries of Charity themselves include many simple, uneducated souls whose understanding of the spirituality for which Mother Teresa stands may be

190

limited, and who find themselves working in areas where they can receive little spiritual guidance in a way which casts yet another dimension on their commitment to poverty. "We are all his humble instruments", Mother Teresa insists repeatedly, and to this must be added her message – ever constructive: "I can do what you can't do. You can do what I can't do. Together we can do something beautiful for God."

The whole – a manifestation of love and joy – is so much greater than the combined sum of its component parts; and in all this the Co-Workers must assume a very special significance for those individuals striving to respond to a personal vision of God and holiness amidst the humdrum activity of their daily lives, for the Co-Workers more obviously perhaps than any other component part of this combined mission are Everyman with his talents, his failings and his foibles facing the challenge to sanctity in a very ordinary world where the gods which present themselves for worship are manifold and not always those of love. As a reflection of the diversity of mankind united in a unique, constructive but by no means inaccessible way, these people of all nationalities, creeds and walks of life are not only working for the brotherhood of man; in a very real and significant sense, they are the brotherhood of man.

# CHAPTER NINE

# THE LEXICON OF LOVE

## "Love is the most universal, the most tremendous and the most mysterious of the cosmic forces."

PIERRE TEILHARD DE CHARDIN

October 7th, 1975 marked the 25th anniversary of the founding of the Missionaries of Charity. Scattered throughout the world, 1,133 Sisters in some eighty houses of the Congregation joined in prayer and thanksgiving with the Co-Workers, the Sick and Suffering, the Brothers and those who offered their lives of contemplation in the seclusion of cloistered monasteries. In Calcutta twenty priests concelebrated a Thanksgiving Mass with the Archbishop of Calcutta for a gathering which had travelled from five continents to assemble beneath the inscription, "I thirst" in the small chapel at Lower Circular Road.

The jubilee mass attended by the Governor of West Bengal was an occasion of supreme joy but it was only one of a series of thanksgiving services which began on 28th September with worship in the American Holy Church of Nazareth and included services in the Methodist Church, the Catholic Cathedral of the Most Holy Rosary, St Paul's Cathedral and the Mar Thomas Syrian Church. Prayers were offered with the Muslims, the Sikhs, the Parsis and the Jains. At the conclusion of a service held in the Buddhist temple, the head monk of the Mahabodhi Society presented Mother Teresa with two electric candles which he said would burn for ever. One of these now forms the light in the Sisters' Sanctuary lamp. At the Assembly of God Church a packed congregation clapped and sang lustily beneath a banner which announced joyfully: "M.C. – 25 years – Christ's Love lives on", and in the Jewish synagogue Mother Teresa was called upon to read the Magnificat before being afforded the singular privilege of entering together with a group of Co-Workers into the "Holy of Holies". Twenty-five years after the first handful of Missionaries of Charity made their step in

*The 25th anniversary of the founding of the Missionaries of Charity was celebrated throughout the world by people of a wide variety of faiths. A ceremony held by the Jains was one of many thanksgiving services in Calcutta.*

the dark into Michael Gomez' "upper room" their mission of love had become one which was distributed throughout the world and one which had apparently won the recognition and acclaim of a variety of religious groups whose shared joy and thanksgiving spoke of a point of reconciliation and inter-

section sometimes forgotten and frequently unvoiced.

In recent years Mother Teresa has been hailed with all the eulogies afforded by the rich and diverse vocabulary of the various faiths. Christians have called her "saint", "divine lady", "one who has done God proud", those more accustomed to the Hindu mode of thinking have chosen to see in her the "reincarnation of Jesus", Muslims have acclaimed her as an "evolved spirit", and people of all religious beliefs and denominations have described her as a "holy person". Asked for his impressions of Mother Teresa, the Muslim President of India Dr Zakir Husain chose to conclude his answer with terminology more readily associated with Christianity:

"We can't handle all the thrown-away children and the dying – especially in places like Calcutta. When she asked for a place to take them away off the streets, we gave her an unused pilgrim rest home, next to the Temple of Kali – the death goddess. Immediately, some Hindu fanatics protested. So we told them, 'Send one of your sisters or mothers into the streets to pick up the dying – your dying Hindus only, if you like, never mind any dying Christians or Moslems. When you do that, we'll send this woman away and you can have your place back.' No one sent anyone, of course. Finally, Mother Teresa picked up a dying Hindu priest who had no place to go and that changed everything . . . In your lexicon, I believe this woman is a saint."

The fact that Dr Husain's answer took the form of an example of what HRH Prince Philip has described as "faith in action" serves significantly to endorse that overworked truism "actions speak louder than words". Compared with the action, the "lexicon" becomes unimportant and inter-changeable. In the course of its history the word "saint" has become laden with associations, some of which are not altogether congenial to the thinking of modern man but, if the vision of the contemporary saint is taken as that of a person of persistently heroic virtue and courage whose life is a model and an inspiration for others, then there are many who are prepared to see Mother Teresa and others like her as saints and these many are members of a variety of faiths. Significantly also their numbers are by no means reduced or restricted by the fact that saints are persons believed to be connected in a special manner with what is viewed as sacred

*"In your lexicon, I believe this woman is a saint."*

reality. Those whose verbal definitions of holiness, goodness or what is sacred are apparently at variance rarely disagree or have difficulty in recognising such qualities when confronted by them in their concrete form – in action.

*"The centipede was happy, quite*
*Until a toad in fun*
*Said, 'Pray, which leg goes after which?'*
*This worked his mind to such a pitch*
*He lay distracted in a ditch*
*Considering how to run"*

A lighthearted verse from the traditions of Zen philosophy illustrates admirably how the introduction of the discursive and the intellectual faculty becomes an impediment to action which was otherwise successfully and harmoniously executed. The same faculty can form a barrier to spirituality. Mother Teresa is non-discursive by nature. Her spirituality is not a question of thinking, reasoning and logic, but of transcending rational thought. She does not come to know God through clear images and careful argument nor with the eyes of the body but with that intuitive inner eye which concerns itself with the ultimate truth at a level where the differences·between religious beliefs break down.

It is possible to look at the spirituality of Mother Teresa and to perceive in it traces of both Buddhist and Hindu mysticism, to detect for example, in her yearning for continual "oneness with Christ" the path which the Buddhist mystic treads towards "nirvana", the realm of enlightenment where he becomes at one with the One; to find in Mother Teresa's self detachment – the process of emptying herself of self – a parallel with the Buddhist "samadhi" with its emphasis on silence, emptiness, the void and the cessation of desire. For Buddhist, Hindu and Christian mystic alike, all insight is the fruit of deep, silent prayer or meditation. For Mother Teresa prayer is a means of intimate contact between her innermost being and God, the Eucharist becomes an ecstatic encounter with Christ.

The complexity of mysticism has called for repeated attempts at definition. In Appendix A of his "Christian Mysticism" Dean Inge provides no less than twenty-six but suffice it here to claim that when religious feeling transcends

*The Missionaries of Charity join in a celebration held in a Sikh temple in honour of the Silver Jubilee.*

its rational content, when the hidden, non-rational, unconscious elements prevail and determine the emotional life and the intellectual attitude the mystical element may be said to have entered into religious experience. At this kind of level – where there is an experience of the immanence of the eternal in the temporal and the temporal in the eternal the search for common ground between Hindu, Christian or Buddhist becomes in a sense unnecessary, for mysticism has its roots in what is the essential material of all religion: a consciousness of a beyond, of something which, though it is interwoven with it, is not of the external world of material phenomena, an awareness of the unseen over and above the seen. At its most developed this awareness can become a unifying factor in a world seeking wholeness. "Though mystical theologies of the East and the West differ widely", writes Evelyn Underhill, "though the ideal of life which they hold out to the soul differ too – yet in the experience of the saint this conflict is seen to be transcended. When the love of God is reached, divergencies become impossible for the soul has passed beyond the sphere of the manifold and is immersed in the one Reality..." "One cannot honestly say", she concludes, "that there are wide differences between the

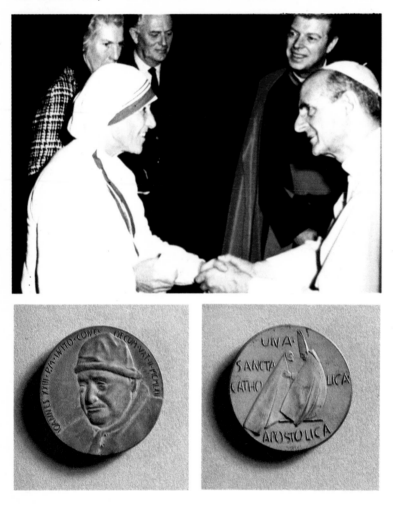

*On March 26th, 1969 the Constitution of the International Association of Co-Workers was presented to Pope Paul VI by Mother Teresa, Mrs Ann Blaikie and her husband, John Blaikie.*

*The papal medal left was given to the International Chairman of the Co-Workers to mark the occasion.*

Brahmin, the Sufi or the Christian mystics at their very best".

In the experience of the saint, that is of someone by whom one lives, who is a revelation of what life is all about and someone too, who has possibly caught a glimpse of the one ultimate Truth – that final synthesis in which all partial truths are resolved – barriers which exist at the intellectual,

198

rational and emotional level diminish in importance in the recognition of what is common to all religions and perhaps too in the realisation that the world would be a poorer place if one creed totally absorbed the rest. The half religious and the irreligious fight about dogma and not the truly religious. The incisive words of Swift: "We have enough religion to hate one another but not enough to love one another" are at times all too apposite but in the truly religious where the quest for wholeness prevails, the result is a supreme tolerance of diversity.

The purpose in drawing on the literature of a variety of faiths and cultures in this book has been to demonstrate in some small way, not that which divides, but that which is common to the brotherhood of man in its shared recognition of goodness and universal quest for truth. From the Rsis, or seers, of the Upanishads down to Tagore and Gandhi, Hindus have acknowledged and proclaimed the fact that truth wears vestures of many colours and speaks in strange tongues. The mystics of numerous other denominations have born witness to the same fact – in the words of Böhme: "Consider the birds in our forests, they praise God each in his own way, in diverse tones and fashions. Think you God is vexed by the diversity and desires to silence discordant voices? All the forms of being are dear to the infinite Being himself" – or of a Sufi verse translated by Professor Browne:

> *"Beaker or flagon, or bowl or jar,*
> *Clumsy or slender, coarse or fine;*
> *However the potter may make or mar,*
> *All were made to contain the wine.*
> *Should we this one or that one shun*
> *When the wine which gives them their worth is one?"*

Mother Teresa's work displays a similar insight: "God has his own ways to work in the hearts of men and we do not know how close they are to him. But by their actions we will always know whether they are at his disposal or not. Whether you are a Hindu, or Muslim or Christian, how you live your life is the proof that you are fully his or not. And we cannot endeavour or judge or pass words that will hurt people. We don't know what way God is appearing to a soul and what way God is drawing that soul, and therefore who are we to condemn anybody?"

There have of course been those who have suggested that the Missionaries of Charity offered food, clothing and medical assistance in exchange for conversion to Christianity. One extremist Hindu, anti-Gandhian group criticised the Nobel choice on the grounds that the efforts of Mother Teresa and the Missionaries of Charity were works of propaganda rather than of selfless service but Mother Teresa has used every available means to show that such accusations are without foundation. There are doubtless those amongst her helpers for whom the kind of tolerance which precludes proselytism represents an almost impossible reversal of much deep-rooted conditioning, but in general the very existence of that extended family of the Co-Workers, compiled as it is of men, women and children of all creeds, colours and castes, speaks more convincingly than any dialectic of that which joins rather than separates mankind. United in their concern – the practical expression of God's love – they have made the simple discovery that by substituting the word God for Christ it becomes possible for people of a wide variety of faiths – be they Hindu, Muslim, Christian or Jew – to join together in prayer. So effective are the results of this discovery that steps have been taken towards the creation of a Hindu Order of "nuns" who would lead the same life as the Missionaries of Charity based on similar vows.

*A stamp issued by the West Bengal Government pays tribute to Mother Teresa's works of love.*

In 1978 a bill entitled with shades of Orwellian "doublespeak", "The Freedom of Religion Bill" was proposed in the Indian parliament. Its ostensible aim was to prevent conversions to Christianity by "force, fraud, inducement or allurement". These terms were so loosely applied, however, that Christian worship and any kind of normal church activity might fall foul of the law. To take only two examples, the suggestion of Divine displeasure was tantamount to "force" while "inducement" included the hope of salvation. The bill formed part of a Government campaign to discourage the activities of foreign missionaries.

Already no foreign missionaries were permitted in tribal areas along the north-eastern border such as Nagaland or Arunachal Pradesh, and many had been expelled or refused extension of their stay in India. The bill which was seen by India's fifteen million Christians as an attempt to put the seal of respectability on discriminatory legislation already enacted in Arunachal Pradesh provoked a strong reaction from church leaders, among them Mother Teresa. The open letter which she wrote to Prime Minister Morarji Desai and members of the Indian Parliament on the subject, because it is so characteristic a voicing of her beliefs, must stand in its entirety:

*Dear Mr Desai and Members of our Parliament*

*After much prayer and sacrifices I write to you, asking you to face God in prayer, before you take the step which will destroy the joy and the freedom of our people.*

*Our people, as you know better than I – are God-fearing people. In whatever way you approach them, that presence of God – the fear of God is there. Today all over the country everybody feels insecure because the very life of freedom of conscience is being touched.*

*Religion is not something that you and I can touch. Religion is the worship of God – therefore, a matter of conscience I alone must decide for myself and you for yourself, what we choose. For me the religion I live and use to worship God is the Catholic Religion. For me this is my very life, my joy and the greatest gift of God in his love to me. He could have given me no greater gift.*

*I love my people very much, more than myself, and so naturally I would wish to give them the joy of possessing this treasure, but it is not mine to give, nor can I force it on any one. So also no man, no law, no Government has the right to prevent me or force me, or any one, if I choose to embrace the religion that gives me peace, joy, love.*

*I was told that Gandhiji had said: "If the Christians would live their lives according to the teaching of Jesus Christ there would be no Hindus left in India." You cannot give what you do not have.*

*This new move that is being brought before the Parliament under the cover of freedom of religion, is false. There is no freedom, if a person is not free to choose according to his or her conscience. Our people in Arunachal are so disturbed. All these years our people have lived together in peace. Now religion is used as a deadly weapon to destory the love they had for each other, just because some are Christians, some Hindus, some Tribals. Are you not afraid of God?*

*You call him ISHWAR, some call him ALLAH, some simple God, but we all have to acknowledge that it is he who made us for greater things; to love and to be loved. Who are we to prevent our people from finding this God who has made them – who loves them – to whom they have to return?*

*You took over your sacred duty in the name of God – acknowledging God's supreme right over our country and her people. It was so beautiful. But now I am afraid for you. I am afraid for our people. Abortion being allowed, has brought so much hatred – for if a mother can murder her own child, what is left for others to kill each other. You do not know what abortion has done and is doing to our people. There is so much more immorality, so many broken homes, so much mental disturbance because of the murder of the innocent unborn child, in the conscience of the unborn child. You don't know how much evil is spreading everywhere.*

*Mr Desai, you are so close to meeting God face to face. I wonder what answer you will give for allowing the destruction of the life of the innocent unborn child and destroying the freedom to serve God, according to one's choice and belief. At the hour of death, I believe we will be judged according to the words of Jesus who has said:*

*"I was hungry, you gave me food*
*I was thirsty, you gave me to drink*
*I was homeless, you took me in*
*I was naked, you clothed me*
*I was sick, you took care of me*
*I was in prison, you visited me.*
*Truly I say to you, for as long as you did it to these*
*the least of my brothers, you did it to me."*

*Gandhiji has also said:*
*"He who serves the poor serves God."*

*I spend hours and hours in serving the sick and the dying, the unwanted, the unloved, the lepers, the mental – because I love God and I believe his word:*

*"You did it to me." This is the only reason and the joy of my life: to love and serve him in the distressing disguise of the poor, the unwanted, the hungry, the thirsty, the naked, the homeless, and naturally in doing, I proclaim his love and compassion for each one of my suffering brothers and sisters.*

*Mr Desai and Members of Parliament, in the name of God, do not destroy the Freedom our country and people have had, to serve and love God according to their conscience and belief. Do not belittle our Hindu Religion saying that our Hindu poor people give up their religion for "a plate of rice". To my knowledge, I have not seen this being done, though we feed thousands of poor people of all caste and creeds though thousands have died in our hands beautifully in peace with God.*

*I remember I picked up a destitute man from the street who was nearly eaten up with maggots. He said gratefully: "I have lived like an animal in the street...but I am going to die like an angel, loved and cared for." And he died a beautiful death, loved and cared for and in peace with God.*

*I have always made it my rule to co-operate whole-heartedly with the Central and State Governments in all undertakings which are for the good of our people.*

*European and Indian Co-Workers work beside the Missionaries of Charity in Shishu Bhavan in an atmosphere which despite the often tragic circumstances of the inmates, remains one of joy.*

*You will be glad to know that we are co-operating very earnestly in helping in family limitation through morally sound means. In Calcutta alone we have 102 centres where families are taught self-control out of love. Here we promote the moral, legal and scientific method of Natural Family Planning. From 1971 to 1978, we have helped 11,701 Hindu families, 5,568 Muslims and 4,341 Christian families. Through this natural and beautiful method there have been 61,397 less babies born.*

*Turning to another sad point, I wish to inform you that I have*

204

In 1975 a medal was issued by the Food and Agriculture Organisation of the United Nations in recognition of Mother Teresa's "exemplary love and concern for the hungry and the poorest of the poor".

Thou shalt work,
But GOD will bless thy labours
Thou shalt walk,
But GOD will bless thy footsteps
Thou shalt suffer,
But GOD will bless thy tears.

Our DAYS.

A beautifully executed parchment was the product of the recognition on the part of one Co-Worker of a particular need for reassurance.

been trying to get into Arunachal Pradesh for some time now, but so far I have not succeeded and yet the Ramakrishna Mission members are entering freely. We are in 87 places in India. Why are we not with our poor in Arunachal?

I pray, and I beg you that you order a day of prayer throughout the country. The Catholics of our country have called an All-India day of fasting, prayer and sacrifice on Friday,

*6th April, to maintain peace and communal harmony and to ensure that India lives up to its noble tradition of religious freedom. I request you to propose a similar day of intercession for all communities of our country – that we may obtain peace, unity and love; that we become one heart, full of love and so become the sunshine of God's love, the hope of eternal happiness and the burning flame of God's love and compassion, in our families, our country and in the world.*

(sd.) *M. Teresa mc*

God bless you

The letter is characteristic in many ways – in its close identification with the Indian people, in its courageous determination, in its emphasis on religion as a matter of individual conscience and in its personal commitment to Roman Catholicism in the context of a tolerant understanding.

*The Indian Government marked the awarding of the Nobel Peace Prize to Mother Teresa, with a special stamp.*

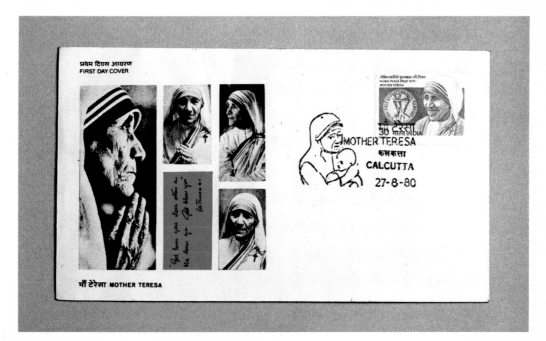

The kind of religious consciousness for which Mother Teresa is so effective a witness may be placed firmly within the context of the 20th century. In 1962 in his book, *The Platonic Tradition in English Thought*, Dean Inge

commented on the movement towards mysticism in the religions of the West: "The centre of gravity in religion has shifted from authority to experience... The fundamental principles of mystical religion are now very widely accepted." The most superficial glance at modern history in relation to the evolution of man must reveal that the human race is in the midst of a crisis point: established political systems are being eroded, hierarchical structures are breaking down and concepts of morality and authority are crumbling – and despite all the negative, destructive accompaniments it is possible to see in the resulting disorder the necessary birthpangs of an unprecedented possibility for the evolution of a true, mature humanity or in the language of Teilhard de Chardin, a "Christed humanity". Man is questioning his nature and role in the cosmos, possibly as never before, and the social questioning of the established order which makes itself all too readily apparent is inevitably and inextricably accompanied by a religious questioning which refuses to be satisfied with dogma, unendorsed by a personal perception of truth, but presented as irrefutable simply because they are dogma, or with the vision of a God residing somewhere above man, dispensing judgement on the basis of clearly and almost simplistically defined concepts of right and wrong, good and evil, heaven and hell.

Bishop Robinson's *Honest to God* was an early voicing of a concept of God not as a being set above and apart from humanity but as the very ground of man's being, to which many now find themselves able to respond. The popularity of books such as *Mr God, this is Anna* which dispensed with the old anthropomorphic image of God with the intuitive vision of a small child: "Mr God ain't got no bum" – speaks for itself. At its most rudimentary man's eternal search for God has ceased to be represented as a journey upwards to a bearded and presumably masculine figure but a journey inwards. The popularity of Buddhism which requires no dogmatic conception of God but is concerned with man's essential divinity, and the appeal of meditation and oriental philosophy particularly among young people of the West may be seen as part of a search for truth which remains unsatisfied by the theologian's understanding of God and man which derives from his faculty for discursive reasoning.

*A point of intersection.* It is possible to see in the "mystical" aspect of Mother

Teresa's spirituality, in her concentration on deep prayer and on that which transcends rational thought, in her emphasis on the intimate relationship between the individual and God which results in all-transcending tolerance and demands great spiritual maturity – that which would answer to the higher form of awareness said to be superseding dogmatic consciousness. Yet it is significant in this context that for her to be a Roman Catholic is everything and that in this respect her orthodoxy is unwavering.

*A meeting of two figures who hold each other in high regard – Pope John Paul II and Mother Teresa.*

Partly perhaps because of the failure of the established Churches to answer the questions which Western society is really asking, recent years have witnessed an unprecedented process of secularisation. The need for some form of renewal to confront the challenge of an increasingly secular lifestyle has made itself increasingly apparent and it is clear to many that profound and far reaching changes in the life and worship of Christians in the Western world must take place sooner or later. The danger is that the positive results of the increased consideration of dogma and doctrine in the perspective of charity may be accompanied by the relaxing of certain Christian disciplines – personal, doctrinal and intellectual to give sanction to a new vision of Christianity in which the authentic action of the modern church is above all else "liberating".

Where responsibility is thrown back more and more upon the individual conscience it is all too easy for renewal to mean the development of a religious life-style which is less and less demanding and more and more anaemic. It was this very danger which Pope John Paul II pinpointed for the benefit of the Vatican Curia in 1976: "Even where Christ is accepted there is at the same time opposition to the full truth of his Person, his mission and his Gospel. There is a desire to 're-shape' him to adapt him to suit mankind in this era of progress and make him fit in with the programme of consumerism and not of transcendental ends. There is opposition to him from these standpoints, and the truth proclaimed and recorded in his name is not tolerated. This opposition to Christ which goes hand-in-hand with paying him lip service – and it is to be found also among those who call themselves his disciples – is particularly symptomatic of our own times."

Mother Teresa's "Lexicon" is very much that of Roman Catholicism. She gives credence only to the official teaching of her Church. Father Le Joly, spiritual adviser to the Sisters has recorded the incident of a newly ordained priest who was sent to give instruction to the Missionaries of Charity. The priest was somewhat disdainful of the traditional beliefs held by the Sisters. Among other things, he claimed there was no need for them to genuflect before the Blessed Sacrament outside the mass, for the presence of Christ was limited to its duration. After he had finished speaking Mother Teresa led the priest to the door, thanked him for coming and informed him that he need not come again. She then spent an hour with the Sisters refuting all that the priest had said and explaining to them the decrees of the Second Vatican Council which reiterated the Roman Catholic Church's traditional doctrine on the Eucharist. Renewal, she insists, can only be properly undertaken within the framework of a discipline which demands the humble surrender of self-will. "The suffering of the Church is caused by liberty and renovation badly understood. We cannot be free except by being able to renounce our will in favour of its. We cannot renew ourselves without having the humility to recognise what must be renewed in ourselves."

The life of Mother Teresa and the Missionaries of Charity is one of complete disposal to Christ's service guaranteed by the discipline of a prayer life which means that each day includes mass, half an hour of meditation, morning prayer, afternoon prayer and an hour of adoration of the sacrament. Of her Co-Workers and Sisters alike, she asks that supreme discipline "pray the work"; and the discipline intensifies rather than inhibits the awareness of the unseen and the eternal. It can be no accident that despite the rigours of their life-style there is no shortage of applicants to join the Missionaries of Charity. At a time when the suggestion is that the search for a God of really archetypal and universal truth to meet the demands of a new awareness and insight, must take place outside the boundaries of the established church, Mother Teresa stands as a remarkable witness to the fact that the discipline of orthodox belief and a highly developed awareness of the transcendant dimension of all existence are not incompatible or in some way mutually exclusive but rather that the one may form a springboard for the other. At a time too when self-realisation is easily confused with the retreat into selfishness she forms a dramatic reminder that if God is within one individual then the same presence cannot and must not be ignored in the next. She is living proof also, that it is possible to experience God deeply and joyfully at the very centre of the difficulties and problems which are inevitably associated with an active life amongst those in whom the presence of God is most vulnerable and most demanding. Like Gandhi she experiences God in the midst of social and religious action and that action is the practical outlet for and response to that greatest of all gifts, love.

Those who have looked at Christianity and rejected it have done so all too frequently not because of what it stands for in principle but because of what Christians have made of it in practice. "Christianity is good, but Christians are bad", proclaimed Romain Rolland. Similarly, Nietzsche, that great exponent of the "God is dead" dictum, pronounced that "there was only ever one real Christian and he was crucified". Of those who professed to be followers of that one real Christian his criticism is renowned: "They would have to sing better songs to me that I might believe in their Redeemer; his disciples would have to look more redeemed." Gandhi who placed so much personal emphasis on the teachings of the Sermon on the Mount was able to admit: "I might perhaps have become a Christian if those I had known had been it twenty-four hours a day."

Christ put mutual love as the specific characteristic of his disciples; Mother Teresa has asked of the Missionaries of Charity and the Co-Workers that they should be conspicuous for the love they bear one another. Similarly Christian unity is all-important "because Christians stand as the light for the other people in the world. If we are Christian then we must be Christ like. Gandhi has said once that if Christians had lived to the full their Christian life there would be no Hindus left in India. So that is what people expect from us, that we live our Christian life to the full." Christian love must radiate outwards – Matthew 19:19 "You shall love your neighbour as yourself" – and it must do so in a way which bears concrete witness to the God from whom it springs – Matthew 5:16 "Let your light so shine before men, that they may see your good works and give glory to your Father who is in heaven." Mother Teresa and those who work with her have endeavoured to do precisely this and their endeavours have won the recognition of the world.

In 1946 Cardinal Gracias, speaking to a gathering of Christians in India, stressed the importance of a practical manifestation on the part of individuals of their belief in God and of charity to all men: "Much concern is expressed nowadays about the future of our community in the new India. My own view is that there cannot be a better safeguard than our own practical appreciation of the religion we profess. All else is secondary. Our religion and culture will be respected in the measure in which each one of us earns the respect of our fellow-countrymen by our practical manifestation of belief in God and in the brotherhood of man, brotherly love towards one and all, irrespective of colour, creed and nationality." In India, where other missions and charitable organisations have at times been confronted by insuperable difficulties and opposition, the Missionaries of Charity known as the "running congregation" because of their speed of action, despite the fact that in the words of a Liverpool Co-Worker "they have had to take some stick", have earned themselves a position of general respect. Mother Teresa is regarded as a national heroine and the Indian government grants her all kinds of privileges in connection with visas and customs exemptions. In 1973 Indira Gandhi gave a free pass on India Airlines to the woman who once offered to work her flight ticket by serving as an air stewardess and who later remained Mrs Gandhi's friend when the rest of the world sat in judgement upon her. To the many other concessions and marks of appreciation such as free travel on Indian Railways must be added the Padma Shri award and the Jawaharlai Nehru Award for International Understanding, presented to her by the Indian Government.

Outside India, world acclaim has found its expression in a string of honorary degrees, medals, awards and prizes culminating in what has been described as the "ultimate accolade", the Nobel Peace Prize.

*Mrs Gandhi pays tribute to a long-standing friend.*

Speaking of the work of the Missionaries of Charity, Mr John Sanness, president of the Nobel Committee chose to reiterate a link, first pinpointed by an Indian journalist, between their lives and those of two other figures who stood for peace in India's history, the Buddha and Gandhi, the father of the Indian nation: "The Sisters, with their serene ways, their saris, their knowledge of local languages, have come to symbolise not only the best in Christian charity, but also the best in Indian culture and civilisation, from Buddha to Ghandhi." The principle may be extended well beyond the boundaries of the Indian nation and its culture. In the words of India's President Giri: "Mother Teresa is among those emancipated souls who have transcended all barriers of race, religion, creed and nation".

When the love of God finds its expression in something that is the concrete reflection of the very best in human nature, then all world views can find in it something which is needed by the brotherhood of man. In the mysterious and un-breakable link between faith and action, Mother Teresa has found the most universal "lexicon" for the most universally needed and universally acclaimed message – a message of love. "Through her self-forgetting service for the poorest of the poor", said Mr Aarvik, vice-chairman of the Nobel Com-mittee, "she has shown something of the finest that man can display at all: the love that does not seek its own, that believes all things, hopes all things, endures all things. And if there is something that our divided world, without peace, needs, then it is people who in the name of Christ will cross boundaries to lessen their neighbour's need, regardless of standing or reputation." To this need only be added Mother Teresa's own insistence that "every work of love brings a person face to face with God".

On 10th December, 1980, in Oslo, in the presence of King Olaf and numerous other dignitaries, a stooping figure dressed in a cotton sari with the now familiar blue border received the Nobel Prize for Peace – an award of £90,000, various donations from the young people of Norway amounting to another £36,000 and a further £3,000 in lieu of the customary celebration banquet, the cancellation of which she had requested in all humility, in order that the money might be used for those who really needed a meal. She accepted this as she had accepted all other honours, as she claimed, "unworthily" but "gratefully in the name of the poor, the hungry, the sick and the lonely". Among those present at the ceremony were representatives not only of the Missionaries of Charity but also of the Co-Workers, and as the cameras of at least seventy photographers flashed and clicked to record an historic moment for the press of the world, those who knew that this kind of experience represented Mother Teresa's greatest trial, willed silently that the pain be taken from her. Tears welled spontaneously in the eyes of a number of Co-Workers; the press commented unanimously on Mother Teresa's "serenity". Before delivering a speech prepared only with a sign of the cross she called upon her audience to recite the Prayer of St Francis and in the name of peace all those present – Roman Catholics, Lutherans, Anglicans, Greek Orthodox, Baptists, Methodists and those who had almost forgotten how to pray – joined in the words "Lord make me an instrument of thy Peace that where there is hatred I may bring love".

*A stooping figure dressed in a cotton sari with the now familiar blue border received the Nobel Prize for Peace.*

The occasion spoke eloquently of many things: of the achievements of those who aspire to nothing, of the recognition long-overdue that the works of love are the works of peace, and linked with that equation, of something profound concerning the true nature of the authority and standing of man. Despite her position at the head of what might be seen as an "empire", Mother Teresa's is a gentle and unobtrusive presence beyond which the suggestion of an unquestionable strength and authority makes itself only quietly apparent. In a world governed by egos she is a living demonstration that authority to be effective does not need to be a thrusting assertion of a greedy self shouting persistently for recognition even under the guise of the search for peace;

*"Let us love others as God has loved each one of us."*

she is also a powerful indication of the direction in which man's real aspirations must lie. "The most telling and profound way of describing the evolution of the universe would undoubtedly be to trace the evolution of love", writes Teilhard de Chardin. Those who carry forward the thrust of evolution are those who by mirroring what is best in mankind – that which gives and that which inspires love – become instrumental in widening and deepening man's knowledge and love of God. Love, according to Pope John Paul II, "is the source that nourishes and the climate in which one grows". That potentially noble fraternity of man will grow in real stature only in proportion to the measure of love shared, given and received by its members. The last word belongs most appropriately and most effectively to Mother Teresa and her Co-Workers:

*My dear Co-Workers,*

*It is with a heart full of gratitude to God and to each one of you that I write this letter. God love you for all the love you have given. In return I can but pray for you more fervently and love you with greater love.*

*Let each of us, as we have resolved to become a true child of God, a carrier of God's love; let us love others as God has loved each one of us, for Jesus has said love one another as I have loved you.*

*Many Christians of the young Church were martyred, because by their actions of love they were recognised to be Christians.*

*Today, the Poor are hungry for bread and rice – and for love and the living word of God.*

> *the Poor are thirsty – for water*
> *and for peace, truth and justice.*

> *the Poor are naked – for clothes, for human dignity*
> *and compassion for the naked sinner.*

> *the Poor are homeless – for a shelter made of bricks,*
> *and for a joyful heart that understands, covers, loves.*

> *they are sick – for medical care –*
> *and for that gentle touch and a warm smile.*

*The "shut-in", the unwanted, the unloved, the alcoholics, the dying destitutes, the abandoned and the lonely, the outcasts and the untouchables, the leprosy sufferers – all those who are a burden to human society – who have lost all hope and faith in life – who have forgotten how to smile – who have lost the sensibility of the warm hand touch of love and friendship – they look to us for comfort – if we turn our back on them, we turn it on Christ, and at the hour of our death we will be judged if we have recognised Christ in them, and on what we have done for and to them. There will only be two ways "come" or "go".*

(sd.) _M. Teresa mc_____

God bless you

*Speech delivered by Professor John Sanness, Chairman of the Norwegian Nobel Committee, on the occasion of the award of the Nobel Peace Prize for 1979, Oslo, December 10, 1979.*

Your Majesty, Your Royal Highnesses, Your Excellencies, Ladies and Gentlemen:

The Norwegian Nobel Committee has awarded the Peace Prize for 1979 to Mother Teresa.

The year 1979 has not been a year of peace: disputes and conflicts between nations, peoples, and ideologies have been conducted with all the accompanying extremes of inhumanity and cruelty. We have witnessed wars, the unrestrained use of violence, we have witnessed fanaticism hand in hand with cynicism, we have witnessed contempt for human life and dignity.

We are faced with new and overwhelming floods of refugees. Not without reason the word genocide has been on many lips. In many countries completely innocent people have been the victims of acts of terror. In this year, moreover, we recall the way in which an entire ethnic group was virtually exterminated in Europe only a generation ago. The Holocaust film series has shaken us, not only as an evil memory from our own not-too-distant past, and as we consider the world of 1979, not one of us can be certain that the like may not recur in the future.

The Norwegian Nobel Committee has considered it right and appropriate, precisely in this year, in their choice of Mother Teresa, to remind the world of the words spoken by Fridtjof Nansen: "Love of one's neighbour is realistic policy".

As a description of Mother Teresa's life's work we might select the slogan that a previous Nobel Peace Prize laureate, Albert Schweitzer, adopted as the leit-motif for his own work: "Veneration for life".

Over the years the Committee has frequently awarded Nobel's Peace Prize to statesmen, men who have carried out their work under the conditions that obtain in our imperfect world. In the opinion of the Committee they had played a dominant role in bringing to an end wars that had already broken out, seeking peaceful solutions to conflicts, and in preventing fresh outbreaks of war.

The Committee has awarded the prize to idealists who explored avenues leading to a better world, in which war would be meaningless or inconceivable and where traditional statesmanship would be superfluous.

The prize has been awarded to individuals and organisations which, through international humanitarian work and co-operation, have been able to contribute to the brotherhood of nations that Alfred Nobel hoped that his Peace Prize would promote.

The prize has been awarded to scientists and organisations dedicated to the task of tackling and overcoming economic and social privation, not least hunger, which is yet another threat to brotherhood and peace. The Committee has awarded the Peace Prize to champions of equality and fraternity among peoples of different races in every country and in every part of the world.

It has awarded the prize to champions of human rights, of the individual man's and woman's claim to the protection of his or her integrity, body and soul, against the power of the State that is so often abused.

There are many paths we can and must pursue to reach our goals – brotherhood and peace.

In awarding Nobel's Peace Prize for 1979 to Mother Teresa the Committee has posed a focal question that we encounter along all these paths: Can any political, social, or intellectual feat of engineering, on the international or on the national plane, however effective and rational, however idealistic and principled its protagonists may be, give us anything but a house built on a foundation of sand, unless the spirit of Mother Teresa inspires the builders and takes its dwelling in their building?

Mother Teresa was born into an Albanian Roman Catholic family in the Yugoslavian town of Skopje. She relates that at the age of twelve she felt a vocation to help the poor. A few years later she listened to accounts of conditions in Bengal, as related by missionaries, and decided there and then that she would work as a missionary in India. At the age of eighteen she joined the Irish Loreto order, whose Sisters ran a mission station in Calcutta. From 1929 to 1946 she taught at the girls' school run by the Order in that city.

It was in 1946 that she applied for permission to go out and work among the poor in the slums of the city. She felt this to be a fresh vocation, a vocation within a vocation, as she herself has expressed it.

She had had a glimpse of the poverty and squalor of the slums, of sick people who remained untended, of lonely men and women lying down to die on the pavement, of the thousands of orphaned children wandering around with no-one to care for them.

It was among these people that she felt a call to work, and to spend the rest of her life, in daily contact with them. She left the sheltered world of the convent and the fashionable girls' school behind her. Her plea to be allowed to go out into the slums and work there was granted. In 1948 she received permission to change from the uniform of the Loreto order to the customary cheap Indian sari. She started her work after an intensive course in nursing.

She was joined by a number of former pupils and other young women. In 1948 this little local community was recognised as a new, separate order, the Missionaries of Charity. In addition to the customary convent vows, a fourth promise, "to give wholehearted, free service to the very poorest", was added.

Fifteen years later, in 1965, Mother Teresa's order was recognised as a papal congregation under the protection of the Vatican. In the years that had elapsed the Missionaries of Charity had witnessed a growth that no-one could have foreseen, and which was to continue. In time, more and more women, Indian as well as foreign, volunteered for this service, and were recruited into the order. It also received the support of an auxiliary organisation consisting of lay helpers. Its activities include slum schools, homes for orphaned children, mobile clinics, leprosy centres, hostels for the dying, food kitchens, vocational training, and much else besides.

In recent years the Order has extended its activities to cover twenty new countries, although the main emphasis is still on India and the neighbouring state of Bangladesh. To date, several million people have benefited from the social welfare and rescue work of the Order.

The Norwegian Nobel Committee is delighted to note this impressive and steadily growing scope of the work undertaken by the Order. It has not, however, attached decisive importance to statistical information: it has not compared such statistics with figures attributable to other organisations and institutions. Many of these have carried out work that merits the greatest respect. Nor has the Committee considered the relationship between private and public activity in the work of redressing and overcoming the physical privation and distress in the world.

The Committee has attached decisive importance to the spirit that has permeated this work. This has been Mother Teresa's fundamental contribution to the Order she has created and run. This it is that explains both why so many people should flock to join the Order, and the interest and respect she has encountered throughout the world. This springs from Mother Teresa's own fundamental attitude to life and her very special personality.

This is clearly and firmly rooted in her Christian faith. She received the first announcement of the award of the Peace Prize with these words: "I accept the prize in the name of the poor. The prize is the recognition of the poor World. Jesus said, 'I am hungry, I am naked, I am homeless'. By serving the poor, I am serving him."

She is merely repeating what she has so often said before: "Actually we are touching Christ's body in the poor. In the poor it is the hungry Christ that we are feeding, it is the naked Christ that we are clothing, it is the homeless Christ that we are giving shelter." Or again: "When I wash that leper's wounds, I feel I am nursing the Lord himself". She sees Christ in every human being, and this in her eyes makes man sacred.

The hallmark of her work has been respect for the individual and the individual's worth and dignity. The loneliest and the most wretched, the dying destitute, the abandoned lepers, have been received by her and her Sisters with warm compassion devoid of condescension, based on this reverence for Christ in Man.

Better than anyone else she has managed to put into practice the recognised fact that gifts de haut en bas, where the recipient has a feeling of one-sided and humiliating dependence on the giver, may prove so hurtful to the recipient's dignity as a human being, that it may well breed bitterness and animosity instead of harmony and peace.

She has arrived at an attitude to the relationship between donor and recipient which eliminates the generally accepted conceptual distinction. In her eyes the person who, in the accepted sense, is the recipient, is also the giver, and the one who gives most. Giving – giving something of oneself – is what confers real joy, and the person who is allowed to give is the one who receives the most precious gift. Where others see clients or customers, she sees fellow-workers, a relationship based not on the expectation of gratitude on the one part, but on mutual understanding and respect, and a warm human and enriching contact.

She and her Sisters regard their work as a cherished duty, and not as a burden. Many visitors have described their first impression of her homes for dying people brought in from the streets, or of the reception centres for outcast lepers. Their first impression is likely to be a harrowing one. But in next to no time they are carried away by the atmosphere of serenity and joy that the Sisters create around them. This is the life of Mother Teresa and her Sisters – a life of strict poverty and long days and nights of toil, a life that affords little room for other joys but the most precious.

A Norwegian poet, whose religious creed was not that of Mother Teresa, has written a poem containing an idea she would have no difficulty in recognising:

> *Life can offer a happiness,*
> *That cannot be turned into grief:*
> *Giving joy to another*
> *Is a joy beyond belief.*

> *There's a sorrow that haunts the world,*
> *And never a tear can abate,*
> *But when you've realised the truth of this*
> *It's already, my friend, too late.*

> *Who can stand all his life by a grave,*
> *Weeping a bitter tear,*
> *With so many hours in the day,*
> *And so many days in the year?*

No hour, no day, is lost for Mother Teresa's Sisters in Calcutta; for them, these are all hours and days of joy.

Mother Teresa's work is grounded in the Christian faith. She has worked among and for people who are not adherents of her religion; she has been a European among Indians, but this has proved no obstacle, and perhaps it would be more correct to say that the work carried out in her spirit has overcome all obstacles.

In 1972 the President of the Republic of India had these words to say about her:

"Mother Teresa is one of those liberated souls who have transcended all barriers presented by race, religion, and nationality. In our present-day troubled world, incessantly plagued by conflict and hatred, the life that is lived and the work that is carried out by people like Mother Teresa bring new hope for the future of mankind."

An Indian journalist wrote recently that "the Sisters with their serene ways, their saris, their knowledge of local languages...have come to symbolise not only the best in Christian charity, but also the best in Indian culture and civilisation, from Buddha to Gandhi, the great saints, the seers, the great lovers of humanity with boundless compassion and consideration for the underprivileged: what Shakespeare called the 'quality of mercy'".

Mother Teresa has personally succeeded in bridging the gulf that exists between the rich nations and the poor nations. Her view of the dignity of man has built a bridge. Unencumbered and naturally she has crossed the gulf by means of this bridge. In India encounters of this kind between people have proved possible: they have been welcomed with open arms, and for this India, too, deserves our appreciation.

Her message has found an echo among people of a different faith: in their tradition, too, we find a groping for the same answers to questions that form part of our human existence.

With her message she is able to reach through to something innate in every human mind – if for no other purpose than to create a potential, a seed for good. If this were not the case, the world would be deprived of hope, and work for peace would have little meaning. It would, furthermore, be incompatible with Mother Teresa's own view of human beings, the men and women she serves because she wishes to serve Christ and draw more close to him.

Mother Teresa once said: "In these twenty years of work among the people, I have come more and more to realise that it is being unwanted that is the worst disease that any human being can ever experience." She believes that the worst disease today is not leprosy or tuberculosis, but rather the feeling of being unwanted, uncared for and deserted by everybody.

It was precisely people in this plight, the poorest of the poor, who were the very first to find warmth and shelter with Mother Teresa. Her intention was to ensure that they enjoyed the feeling of being received and recognised as people with their own human dignity and the right to respect.

Mother Teresa works in the world as she finds it, in the slums of Calcutta and other towns and cities. But she makes no distinction between poor and rich persons, between poor and rich countries. Politics have never been her concern, but economic, social, and political work with these same aims are in complete harmony with her own life's work.

In our endeavours, on the national as on the international level, we have a lesson to learn from her work for individuals in distress. On the international level our efforts can only serve the cause of peace if they do not offend the self-respect of the poor nations. All aid given by the rich countries must be given in the spirit of Mother Teresa.

There would be no better way of describing the intentions that have motivated the decision of the Norwegian Nobel Committee than the comment of the President of the World Bank, Robert Macnamara, when he declared: "Mother Teresa deserves Nobel's Peace Prize because she promotes peace in the most fundamental manner, by her confirmation of the inviolability of human dignity".

As we have gathered here together to thank God for the Nobel Peace Prize, I think it will be beautiful that we pray the prayer of St Francis of Assisi which always surprises me very much. We pray this prayer every day after Holy Communion, because it is very fitting for each one of us. And I always wonder that 400-500 years ago when St Francis of Assisi composed this prayer, they had the same difficulties that we have today as we compose this prayer that fits very nicely for us also. I think some of you already have got it – so we will pray together:

Let us thank God for the opportunity that we all have together today, for this gift of peace that reminds us that we have been created to live that peace, and that Jesus became man to bring that good news to the poor. He, being God, became man in all things like us except in sin, and he proclaimed very clearly that he had come to give the good news.

The news was peace to all of good will and this is something that we all want – the peace of heart. And God loved the world so much that he gave his son – it was a giving; it is as much as if to say it hurt God to give, because he loved the world so much that he gave his son. He gave him to the Virgin Mary, and what did she do with him?

As soon as he came in her life, immediately she went in haste to give that good news, and as she came into the house of her cousin, the child – the unborn child – the child in the womb of Elizabeth, lept with joy. He was, that little unborn child was, the first messenger of peace. He recognised the Prince of Peace, he recognised that Christ had come to bring the good news for you and for me. And as if that was not enough – it was not enough to become a man – he died on the cross to show that greater love, and he died for you and for me and for that leper and for that man dying of hunger and that naked person lying in the street not only of Calcutta, but of Africa, and New York, and London, and Oslo – and insisted that we love one another as he loves each one of us. And we read that in the Gospel very clearly: "love as I have loved you; as I love you; as the Father has loved me, I love you." And the harder the Father loved him, he gave him to

us, and how much we love one another, we too must give to each other until it hurts.

It is not enough for us to say: "I love God, but I do not love my neighbour." St John says that you are a liar if you say you love God and you don't love your neighbour. How can you love God whom you do not see, if you do not love your neighbour whom you see, whom you touch, with whom you live? And so this is very important for us to realise that love, to be true, has to hurt.

It hurt Jesus to love us. It hurt him. And to make sure we remember his great love, he made himself the bread of life to satisfy our hunger for his love – our hunger for God – because we have been created for that love. We have been created in his image. We have been created to love and be loved, and he has become man to make it possible for us to love as he loved us. He makes himself the hungry one, the naked one, the homeless one, the sick one, the one in prison, the lonely one, the unwanted one, and he says: "You did it to me". He is hungry for our love, and this is the hunger of our poor people. This is the hunger that you and I must find. It may be in our own home.

I never forget an opportunity I had in visiting a home where they had all these old parents of sons and daughters who had just put them in an institution and forgotten, maybe. And I went there, and I saw in that home they had everything, beautiful things, but everybody was looking toward the door. And I did not see a single one with a smile on their face. And I turned to the sister and I asked: How is that? How is it that these people who have everything here, why are they all looking toward the door? Why are they not smiling.

I am so used to see the smiles on our people, even the dying ones smile. And she said: "This is nearly every day. They are expecting, they are hoping that a son or daughter will come to visit them. They are hurt because they are forgotten." And see – this is where love comes. That poverty comes right there in our own home, even neglect to love. Maybe in our own family we have somebody who is feeling lonely, who is feeling sick, who is feeling worried, and these are difficult days for everybody. Are we there? Are we there to receive them? Is the mother there to receive the child?

I was surprised in the West to see so many young boys and girls given into drugs. And I tried to find out why. Why is it like that? And the answer was: "Because there is no one in the family to receive them". Father and mother are so busy they have no time. Young parents are in some institution and the child goes back to the street and gets involved in something. We are talking of peace. These are things that break peace.

But I feel the greatest destroyer of peace today is abortion, because it is a direct war, a direct killing, direct murder by the mother herself. And we read in the scripture, for God says very clearly: "Even if a mother could forget her child, I will not forget you. I have curved you in the palm of my hand." We are curved in the palm of his hand; so close to him, that unborn child has been curved in the hand of God. And that is what strikes me most, the beginning of that sentence, that even if a mother *could* forget, something impossible – but even if she could forget – I will not forget you.

And today the greatest means, the greatest destroyer of peace is abortion. And we who are standing here – our parents wanted us. We would not be here if our parents would do that to us.

Our children, we want them, we love them. But what of the other millions. Many people are very, very concerned with the children of India, with the children of Africa where quite a number die, maybe of malnutrition, of hunger and so on, but millions are dying deliberately by the will of the mother. And this is what is the greatest destroyer of peace today. Because if a mother can kill her own child, what is left for me to kill you and you to kill me? There is nothing between.

And this I appeal in India, I appeal everywhere – "Let us bring the child back" – and this year being the child's year: What have we done for the child? At the beginning of the year I told, I spoke everywhere and I said: Let us ensure this year that we make every single child born, and unborn, wanted. And today is the end of the year. Have we really made the children wanted?

I will tell you something terrifying. We are fighting abortion by adoption. We have saved thousands of lives. We have sent word to all the clinics, to the hospitals, police stations: "Please don't destroy the child; we will take the child". So every hour of the day and night there is always somebody – we have quite a number of unwedded mothers – tell them: "Come, we will take care of you, we will take the child from you, and we will get a home for the child". And we have a tremendous demand for families who have no children, that is the blessing of God for us. And also, we are doing another thing which is very beautiful. We are teaching our beggars, our leprosy patients, our slum dwellers, our people of the street, natural family planning.

And in Calcutta alone in six years – it is all in Calcutta – we have had 61,273 babies less from the families who would have had them because they practice this natural way of abstaining, of self-control, out of love for each other. We teach them the temperature method which is very beautiful, very simple. And our poor people understand. And you know what they have told me? "Our family is healthy, our family is united, and we can have a baby whenever we want". So clear – those people in the street, those beggars – and I think that if our people can do like that how much more you and all the others who can know the ways and means without destroying the life that God has created in us.

The poor people are very great people. They can teach us so many beautiful things. The other day one of them came to thank us and said: "You people who have evolved chastity, you are the best people to teach us family planning because it is nothing more than self-control out of love for each other." And I think they said a beautiful sentence. And these are people who maybe have nothing to eat, maybe they have not a home where to live, but they are great people.

The poor are very wonderful people. One evening we went out and we picked up four people from the street. And one of them was in a most terrible condition. And I told the Sisters: "You take care of the other three; I will take care of this one that looks worse". So I did for her all that my love can do. I put her in bed, and there was such a beautiful smile on her face. She took hold of my hand, as she said one word only: "thank you" – and she died.

I could not help but examine my conscience before her. And I asked: "What would I say if I was in her place?" And my answer was very simple. I would have tried to draw a little attention to myself. I would have said: "I am hungry, I am dying, I am cold, I am in pain", or something. But she gave me much more – she gave me her grateful love. And she died with a smile on her face – like that man who we picked up from the drain, half eaten with worms, and we brought him to the home – "I have lived like an animal in the street, but I am going to die like an angel, loved and cared for." And it was so wonderful to see the greatness of that man who could speak like that, who could die like that without blaming anybody, without cursing anybody, without comparing anything. Like an angel – this is the greatness of our people.

And that is why we believe what Jesus has said: "I was hungry, I was naked, I was homeless; I was unwanted, unloved, uncared for – and you did it to me."

I believe that we are not really social workers. We may be doing social work in the eyes of the people. But we are really contemplatives in the heart of the world. For we are touching the body of Christ twenty-four hours. We have twenty-four hours in his presence, and so you and I. You too must try to bring that presence of God into your family, for the family that prays together stays together. And I think that we in our family, we don't need bombs and guns, to destroy or to bring peace – just get together, love one another, bring that peace, that joy, that strength of presence of each other in the home. And we will be able to overcome all the evil that is in the world. There is so much suffering, so much hatred, so much misery, and we with our prayer, with our sacrifice are beginning at home. Love begins at home, and it is not how much we do, but how much love we put in the action that we do. It is to God almighty – how much we do does not matter, because he is infinite, but how much love we put in that action. How much we do to him in the person that we are serving.

Some time ago in Calcutta we had great difficulty in getting sugar. And I don't know how the word got around to the children, and a little boy of four years old, a Hindu boy, went home and told his parents: "I will not eat sugar for three days. I will give my sugar to Mother Teresa for her children." After three days his father and mother brought him to our house. I had never met them before, and this little one could scarcely pronounce my name. But he knew exactly what he had come to do. He knew that he wanted to share his love.

And this is why I have received such a lot of love from all. From the time that I have come here I have simply been surrounded with love, and with real, real understanding love. It could feel as if everyone in India, everyone in Africa is somebody very special to you. And I felt quite at home, I was telling Sister today. I feel in the convent with the Sisters as if I am in Calcutta with my own Sisters. So completely at home here, right here.

And so here I am talking with you. I want you to find the poor here, right in your own home first. And begin love there. Be that good news to your own people. And find out about your next-door neighbour. Do you know who they are?

I had the most extraordinary experience with a Hindu family who had eight children. A gentleman came to our house and said: "Mother Teresa, there is a family with eight children; they have not eaten for so long; do something". So I took some rice and I went there immediately. And I saw the children – their eyes shining with hunger. I don't know if you have ever seen hunger. But I have seen it very often. And she took the rice, she divided the rice, and she went out. When she came back I asked her: "Where did you go, what did you do?" And she gave me a very simple answer: "They are hungry also". What struck me most was that she knew – and who are they? a Muslim family – and she knew. I didn't bring more rice that evening because I wanted them to enjoy the joy of sharing.

But there were those children, radiating joy, sharing the joy with their mother because she had the love to give. And you see this is where love begins – at home. And I want you – and I am very grateful for what I have received. It has been a tremendous experience and I go back to India – I will be back by next week, the 15th I hope, and I will be able to bring your love.

And I know well that you have not given from your abundance, but you have given until it has hurt you. Today the little children, they gave – I was so surprised – there is so much joy for the children that are hungry. That the children like themselves will need love and get so much from their parents.

So let us thank God that we have had this opportunity to come to know each other, and that this knowledge of each other has brought us very close. And we will be able to help the children of the whole world, because as you know our

Sisters are all over the world. And with this prize that I have received as a prize of peace, I am going to try to make the home for many people that have no home. Because I believe that love begins at home, and if we can create a home for the poor, I think that more and more love will spread. And we will be able through this understanding love to bring peace, be the good news to the poor. The poor in our own family first, in our country and in the world.

To be able to do this, our Sisters, our lives have to be woven with prayer. They have to be woven with Christ to be able to understand, to be able to share. Today there is so much suffering and I feel that the passion of Christ is being relived all over again. Are we there to share that passion, to share that suffering of people – around the world, not only in the poor countries. But I found the poverty of the West so much more difficult to remove.

When I pick up a person from the street, hungry, I give him a plate of rice, a piece of bread, I have satisfied. I have removed that hunger. But a person that is shut out, that feels unwanted, unloved, terrified, the person that has been thrown out from society – that poverty is so hurtful and so much, and I find that very difficult. Our Sisters are working amongst that kind of people in the West.

So you must pray for us that we may be able to be that good news. We cannot do that without you. You have to do that here in your country. You must come to know the poor. Maybe our people here have material things, everything, but I think that if we all look into our own homes, how difficult we find it sometimes to smile at each other, and that the smile is the beginning of love.

And so let us always meet each other with a smile, for the smile is the beginning of love, and once we begin to love each other, naturally we want to do something. So you pray for our Sisters and for me and for our Brothers, and for our Co-Workers that are around the world. Pray that we may remain faithful to the gift of God, to love him and serve him in the poor together with you. What we have done we would not have been able to do if you did not share with your prayers, with your gifts, this continual giving. But I don't want you to give me from your abundance. I want that you give me until it hurts.

The other day I received $15 from a man who has been on

his back for twenty years and the only part that he can move is his right hand. And the only companion that he enjoys is smoking. And he said to me: "I do not smoke for one week, and I send you this money". It must have been a terrible sacrifice for him but see how beautiful, how he shared. And with that money I brought bread and I gave to those who are hungry with a joy on both sides. He was giving and the poor were receiving.

This is something that you and I can do – it is a gift of God to us to be able to share our love with others. And let it be able to share our love with others. And let it be as it was for Jesus. Let us love one another as he loved us. Let us love him with undivided love. And the joy of loving him and each other – let us give now that Christmas is coming so close.

Let us keep that joy of loving Jesus in our hearts, and share that joy with all that we come in touch with. That radiating joy is real, for we have no reason not to be happy because we have Christ with us. Christ in our hearts, Christ in the poor that we meet, Christ in the smile that we give and the smile that we receive. Let us make that one point – that no child will be unwanted, and also that we meet each other always with a smile, especially when it is difficult to smile.

I never forget some time ago about fourteen professors came from the United States from different universities. And they came to Calcutta to our house. Then we were talking about the fact that they had been to the home for the dying. (We have a home for the dying in Calcutta, where we have picked up more than 36,000 people only from the streets of Calcutta, and out of that big number more than 18,000 have died a beautiful death. They have just gone home to God.) And they came to our house and we talked of love, of compassion. And then one of them asked me: "Say, Mother, please tell us something that we will remember". And I said to them: "Smile at each other, make time for each other in your family. Smile at each other."

And then another one asked me: "Are you married?" And I said: "Yes, and I find it sometimes very difficult to smile at Jesus because he can be very demanding sometimes". This is really something true. And there is where love comes – when it is demanding, and yet we can give it to him with joy.

Just as I have said today, I have said that if I don't go to heaven for anything else I will be going to heaven for all the publicity because it has purified me and sacrificed me and made me really ready to go to heaven.

I think that this is something, that we must live life beautifully, we have Jesus with us and he loves us. If we could only remember that God loves us, and we have an opportunity to love others as he loves us, not in big things, but in small things with great love, then Norway becomes a nest of love. And how beautiful it will be that from here a centre for peace from war has been given. That from here the joy of life of the unborn child comes out. If you become a burning light of peace in the world, then really the Nobel Peace Prize is a gift of the Norwegian people. God bless you!

*The Citation for the Templeton Award*
*for Progress in Religion*
*awarded to Mother Teresa*
*in April 1973*

"Mother Teresa has been instrumental
in widening and deepening man's knowledge
and love of God
and thereby furthering the quest
for the quality of life
that mirrors the divine."

# TEMPLETON AWARD SPEECH

Dear Co-Workers for Christ, we are here today to thank God for giving grace to Mr Templeton to accept, to give of his best, to be spent to the glory of God. You have accepted that vision to appreciate the gift of God. And so today and now we thank God that he had the courage to give, to be spent for the glory of God, the fund that he had received so generously from God. In giving this award to me, actually it is given to the people, to all those who share with me throughout the world in the work of love, in spreading God's love amongst men.

Actually we are touching his body. It is the hungry Christ that we are feeding, it is the naked Christ that we are clothing, it is the homeless Christ that we are giving shelter and it is not just hunger for bread, and nakedness for cloth, and homelessness for a house made of bricks but Christ today is hungry in our poor people, and even in the rich, for love, for being cared for, for being wanted, for having someone to call their own.

Today, like before, when Jesus comes amongst his own, his own don't know him. He comes in the rotten bodies of our poor, he comes even in the rich, who are being suffocated with their riches, in the loneliness of their hearts, and there is no one to love them. And here Jesus comes to you and to me. And often, very, very often, we pass him by.

Here in England, and in other places such as Calcutta, we find lonely people who are known by the number of their room. Where are we then? Do we really know that there are some people, maybe next door to us? Maybe there is a blind man who would be happy if you would read the newspaper for him. Maybe there is a rich person who has no one to visit him. He has plenty of other things but he is nearly drowned in them. There is no touch; and he needs your touch. Some time back, a very rich man came to our place and he told me: "this I give you for somebody to come to my house. I am nearly half blind, and my wife is nearly mental, and our children have all gone abroad. And we are dying of loneliness." They are longing for the loving sound of a human voice.

And in one of the places in Melbourne, I visited an old man, whom nobody ever knew that he existed, and I saw his room, in a terrible state, and I wanted to clean his house, his room, and he kept on saying, "I'm all right", but I didn't say a word, in the end he allowed me.

There in that room was a beautiful lamp, covered with dirt, many years. I asked him: "Why do you not light the lamp?" – "For whom", he said, "No one comes for me, I don't need the lamp". And I asked him: "Will you light the lamp, if the Sisters come to see you?" he said, "Yes, if I hear a human voice, I will do it". And the other day, he sent me word: "Tell my friend the light she has lighted in my life is still burning".

This is the people that we must know. This is Jesus yesterday and today and tomorrow and you and I must know who they are. That knowledge will lead us to love them. And love the service. Let us not be satisfied with just paying money. Money is not enough. Money can be got – but they need your hands to serve them, they need your hearts to love them. And this award is for spreading religion – to me and to you. The religion of Christ is love, of spreading love first of all in your own home, maybe your children, maybe your wife or husband, maybe your neighbour – love the things at home.

Our Sisters are working now in eight countries, facing many calamities where people are suffering so much but there is something very beautiful in our poor people. They are so grateful. They are so lovable. They are so dedicated with their love. You have to know them. And we can know them only if we come to them.

Very often I ask people to come to our home for the dying. We have a big place in Calcutta and in the twenty-one years we have picked up over 27,000 people from the streets. And I ask the people not to come and to give things – things I can get for the asking – but I want their presence, just to touch them, just to smile at them, just to be present with them, it means such a lot for our people.

The same thing for our lepers, the same thing for our crippled, unloved, uncared for children. It is the same thing. They need love, they need their compassion, they need their touch. And at least that is the Host during Mass. When he touches the Body of Christ on the altar, it is with that touch, with that love, with that faith, we are to touch the body of Christ in the poor, because he cannot deceive us. It is the same Jesus who met Saul going to Damascus, who was on his way to disturb, to kill, to destroy the Christians and he asked; "Saul, Saul why hast thou foresaken me?" and Saul asked; "Who art thou, Lord?". "I am Jesus Christ thou persecutest."

And today, it is the same Christ, the same Jesus, the same today in our poor people, who are unwanted, unemployed, uncared for, hungry and naked and homeless. They are useless to the state or to society, and nobody has time for them. And it is you and I as Christians who, worthy of that love of Christ, if our love is true, must find them. We must help them, they are there for the finding.

And here in this city – great city – of London, there is so much – so much that you and I can do. The first time I was here in London, we went out at night. It was a terrible, cold night and we found the people on the street. And there was an old man, well-spoken man, shivering with cold. He was in front of me. In front of him there was another old man – a negro man – with his coat open. He was protecting him from the cold.

This gentleman was saying: "Take me, take me any-where, I am longing to sleep between two sheets". He was a well-spoken man and must have had better days. But there he was. And we looked around and we could see many. Not as many as in Calcutta, not as many, maybe as in other places, but here there are many. If there is just one, he is Jesus, he is the one that is hungry for love, for care. And as it is written in the scripture: "I looked for one to care for me and I couldn't find him". How terrible it would be if Jesus had to say that to us today, after dying for us on the cross.

# THE VOCATION OF THE
## MISSIONARIES OF CHARITY

The Missionaries of Charity grew from small beginnings. The Society sprang from a simple response to the sufferings of human beings in a great city.

First one woman, Mother Teresa, then a little band of young volunteers, went out on the streets of Calcutta. A million refugees thronged the city, which lacked food, shelter and all resources for them. Earlier, a dreadful famine had dislocated the life of Calcutta and the surrounding province of Bengal.

Mother Teresa started in 1948 with a slum school to teach the children of the poor. In 1949, some of her former pupils joined her. As Sister Teresa, a Sister of Loreto, Mother Teresa had been a teacher for twenty years. When they found men, women and children dying on the streets they took them to hospitals, sometimes in a wheelbarrow. When the hospitals, already full, had to turn them away, the group rented a room so that they could care for helpless people otherwise condemned to die in the gutter.

*"In the choice of works",* explained Mother Teresa, *"there was neither planning, nor preconceived ideas. We started our work as the sufferings of the people called us. God showed us what he wanted us to do."*

In 1950, the group was established by the Church as a Diocesan Congregation of the Calcutta Diocese. It was known as the Missionaries of Charity. The spirit was that of seeing Jesus in every person, in the "distressing disguise", especially of the poorest person, of the person dying in the gutter or suffering from leprosy. The Sisters took, in addition to the three vows of poverty, chastity and obedience, a fourth vow:

*"To give whole-hearted and free service to the poorest of the poor."*

To be able to understand the poor, the Sisters choose poverty which has become, says Mother Teresa, *"their freedom, joy and strength"*.

Schools were started to give free instruction to street and slum children. A Home for the Dying was opened in 1952 in space made available by the Corporation of Calcutta, namely the Pilgrims' Hostel of the Temple of Kali. Shortly afterwards, a home was opened for children found abandoned and dying. Soon there were enough Sisters to open Mother and Child Clinics, and eventually a mobile medical service for groups of people suffering from leprosy.

The Congregation of Missionaries of Charity was recognised by the Vatican as a Pontifical Congregation in 1965.

The Missionaries of Charity could then begin work outside India. Already there were communities of the Missionaries of Charity in most of the large cities of India. Invitations to work for the poor came to the Missionaries of Charity from corners of need in the entire world. Only when the invitation came from the local Bishop, could the Sisters respond. Communities of Missionaries of Charity moved among the sick, the needy and unwanted in over thirty countries in Asia, Australia, Africa, Latin America, Central America, Europe and North America.

The Missionary Brothers of Charity, founded in 1963, are working in Calcutta and other cities of India as well as in several countries overseas.

The Co-Workers of Mother Teresa were affiliated with the Missionaries of Charity in 1969.

The same commitment illumines the work of the Sisters and Brothers everywhere in the world, namely:

*To love Christ with undivided love in chastity, through freedom of poverty, in total surrender in obedience, and whole-hearted and free service to the poorest of the poor.*

What is a Co-Worker?

A Co-Worker of Mother Teresa is one who chooses a way of life that calls for seeing God in every human being – in seeing God in everyone, starting with those closest to us, we become ready to share ourselves with the lonely, the ill, the bereaved, the poor and the unwanted and unloved. We are strengthened by being part of a world wide company of those who bear witness to the presence of God in every member of the family of man.

How does one become a Co-Worker?

We become a Co-Worker simply by wanting to be one. It

is not an "organisation" in the ordinary sense of the word, but rather a family whose members seek to come closer to God and to each other through prayer and loving service to their fellow men. Mother Teresa keeps in touch with her Co-Workers through Newsletters which are circulated among Co-Workers.

How may one serve as an active Co-Worker?

Mother Teresa desires her Co-Workers to maintain deep family love in the home, and beyond that, to seek to serve those in need in their own neighbourhood, their town, their country, the world. Mother Teresa asks that we find "those who need us" and get to know them personally. She tells us:

*We must go to those who have no one, to those who suffer from the worst disease of all, the disease of being unwanted, unloved, uncared for.*

Mother Teresa reminds her Co-Workers that *"it is only when we know the people that we can understand and love them".* She asks the Co-Workers to do the "little things", the things no one else has time for. Thus many Co-Workers have formed loving relationships with those in hospitals, geriatric homes, prisons and homes for the physically and mentally handicapped, with the bereaved or with the elderly who wait day after lonely day for the compassionate touch of a friend.

At Mother Teresa's suggestion Co-Workers come together regularly for one hour of prayer and meditation. She says:

*You will come closer to God, to each other and to the people through this hour.*

And so across the world, informal communities of Co-Workers (the young and old, rich and poor, able and disabled) meet for this hour with God and with each other.

Furthermore, the Co-Workers by whatever practical means support the Missionaries of Charity in their mission of love to the poorest of the poor wherever they are found.

THE LINK WITH THE SICK AND SUFFERING
Mother Teresa writes:

*I want especially the paralysed, the cripples, the incurables to join – how happy I am to have you all – often when the work*

247

*is very hard I think of each one of you, and tell God — look at my suffering children and for their love bless this work. You are a Treasure House, The Power House of the Missionaries of Charity.*

Sister and Brothers can be "adopted spiritually" by a Sick or Suffering Co-Worker, and the Sisters or Brothers in their turn will pray for their Sick and Suffering Links.

## LINKS WITH THE CONTEMPLATIVE ORDERS

Mother Teresa has asked the Co-Workers to organise a "Spiritual Linking" between the Convents of the Missionaries of Charity around the world and the Religious Houses of Contemplative Communities. She believes in the dogma of the Communion of Saints. She well knows that the apostolate of the Missionaries of Charity would be sterile if not reinforced by prayer and sacrifice. Any religious houses who would be prepared to take "Spiritual care" of one of the Communities of the Missionaires of Charity should write for further information.

## VOCATIONS

Candidates who wish to join can be rich or poor and of any nationality. The qualities needed are that one be:

— Guided by the right intention.
— Desirous to serve the poor according to the Constitutions and to live and work as a Missionary of Charity.
— Healthy in body and mind and able to bear hardships.
— Able to acquire knowledge; of a cheerful disposition; and able to exercise sound judgement.
— Possessed of a good sense of humour.

The Spirit of the Society is one of Total Surrender, Loving Trust and Cheerfulness.

## THE CO-WORKER'S WAY OF LIFE

*The Co-Worker's Way of Life is a Way of Love*

1. The International Association of "Co-Workers of Mother Teresa" consists of men, women, young people and children of all religions and denominations throughout the world, who seek to love God in their fellow men through whole-hearted free service to the poorest of the poor of all castes and

creeds, and who wish to unite their lives progressively in the spirit of prayer and sacrifice with the work of Mother Teresa and the Missionaries of Charity.

2. The aim of the International Association is to help its members:—

(a) To recognise God in the person of the poor and to love him better through works of charity and service to the poor.

(b) To know the poor. Knowledge leads to love, and love to service. And so all Co-Workers should give their hearts to love them and their hands to serve them.

(c) To radiate love and compassion in their homes, communities and their surroundings.

(d) To form, where possible, communities of Co-Workers desirous of sharing more deeply in the life of sacrifice and work of the Missionaries of Charity.

3. The "poorest of the poor" are the hungry, the thirsty, the naked, the homeless, the ignorant, the captives, the crippled, the leprosy sufferers, the alcoholics and drug addicts, the dying destitutes and the bereaved, the unloved, the abandoned, the outcasts and all those who are a burden to human society, who have lost all hope and faith in life.

4. The Co-Workers recognise the dignity, the individuality and the infinite value of every human life.

5. Christ, being rich, became poor for love of us, and since we are trying to live a life of love in action, we too should free ourselves from all that is binding and love one another as He loves us.

6. At the same time and in the same spirit, Co-Workers make available to the Missionaries of Charity whatever time, and material and spiritual help are within their power to provide, and offer their God-given talents in the service of the poor.

7. As the Missionaries of Charity give whole-hearted free service to the poor, so do the Co-Workers with love and joy.

8. The Sick and Suffering Co-Workers and those unable to join in activities may become linked with an individual Sister or Brother by offering their prayers and suffering for such a Brother or Sister, and supported where possible by the Co-Workers.

9. Contemplative Orders may be linked in prayer with Communities of the Missionaries of Charity.

10. All money donated to the Missionaries of Charity should

be sent to them and it will be used according to the intentions of the donor for the poor served by the Missionaries of Charity.

## LIFE OF PRAYER

1. Let us learn to pray the work by doing it in his presence; by doing it with him, for him and to him all the 24 hours.
2. Co-Workers of Mother Teresa unite with the Missionaries of Charity by praying the daily prayer.
3. Co-Workers should be encouraged to have one hour of prayer and meditation together at least once a month.
4. An Annual Day of Prayer and Thanksgiving will be held on 7th October throughout the world, being the day on which the Society of the Missionaries of Charity was founded in 1950. On that day all are asked to unite with the Sisters and Brothers in giving thanks to God.

## LIFE OF LOVE IN ACTION

1. All Co-Workers express their love of God through service to the poor as Jesus Christ himself has said: "Whatever you did to the least of these my brethren, you did it to me". (Matt. 25:40). "For I was hungry and you gave me to eat, I was thirsty and you gave me to drink. I was homeless and you took me in, naked and you clothed me, in prison and you came to see me." (Matt. 25:35).
2. In answer to Christ's plea to love one another as he has loved us, Co-Workers should become sensitive and responsive to the needs of their family, their next door neighbour, those in their street, in their town, their country, and the whole world. Co-Workers, by putting their understanding love into action, no matter how small the action may be, will thus share in the "wholehearted free service to the poor" which the Sisters and Brothers vow to God.
3. Informal Communities of Co-Workers, by their understanding love for one another, their joyful spirit and life of love and service, will show forth in their neighbourhoods the way to peace and joy.
4. The keynotes of the giving are Love and Service.

# THE CO-WORKERS' PRAYER

Make us worthy, Lord, to serve our fellow men throughout the world who live and die in poverty and hunger.

Give them, through our hands, this day their daily bread; and by our understanding love, give peace and joy.

Lord, make me a channel of thy peace; that where there is hatred, I may bring love; that where there is wrong, I may bring the spirit of forgiveness; that where there is discord, I may bring harmony; that where there is error, I may bring truth; that where there is doubt, I may bring faith; that where there is despair, I may bring hope; that where there are shadows, I may bring light; that where there is sadness, I may bring joy.

Lord, grant that I may seek rather to comfort than to be comforted; to understand than to be understood; to love than to be loved; for it is by forgetting self that one finds; it is by forgiving that one is forgiven; it is by dying that one awakens to eternal life. Amen.

Oh God, the father of all,
You ask everyone of us to spread
Love where the poor are humiliated,
Joy where the Church is brought low,
And reconciliation where people are divided...
Father against son, mother against daughter,
Husband against wife,
Believers against those who cannot believe,
Christians against their unloved fellow Christians.

You open this way for us, so that the wounded body of
Jesus Christ, your Church, may be leaven of Communion
for the poor of the earth and in the whole human family.

*A prayer compiled by Mother Teresa in conjunction with
Brother Roger of Taizé, seen on these pages during a
visit to Calcutta.*

Offers of help and enquiries relating to the work of Mother Teresa, the Missionaries of Charity and the Co-Workers should be addressed to:

The Missionary Sisters of Charity

149 George Street
Fitzroy 3065
Melbourne, Victoria
AUSTRALIA
or
26 Islampur Road
Dacca-1
BANGLADESH
or
177 Bravington Road
London W9
ENGLAND
or
c/o Jesuit House
P.O. Box 32778
Nairobi
KENYA
or
5 Rue Balisage
Roche Bois
Port Louis
MAURITIUS
or
P.O. Box 82
Port Moresby
Hanubade
PAPUA, NEW GUINEA
or
c/o Archbishop's House
Private Bag
Tabora
TANZANIA
or
335 East 145th Street
Bronx
New York 10451
U.S.A.

or
54a Lower Circular Road
Calcutta-700016
WEST BENGAL

The Missionary Brothers of Charity

185 Prince Edward Road 8/A
Kowloon
HONG KONG
or
1-39-3 Nihontsutsum
Daitoh-Ku
Tokyo 111
JAPAN
or
235 Winston Street
Los Angeles
California 90013
U.S.A.
or
7 Mansatala Row
Calcutta 700 023
WEST BENGAL

The Missionary Sisters of the Word (Contemplatives)

1070 Union Avenue
Bronx
New York 10459
U.S.A.

The Missionary Brothers of the Word (Contemplatives)

Via Agapito 8A
Rome 00177
ITALY

The Chairman of the Co-Workers for any of the countries
mentioned and for any neighbouring countries can also be
contacted c/o the addresses above.

The International Link, Mrs Ann Blaikie, may be contacted through the Missionaries of Charity in London, the Link for the Sick and Suffering, Mlle Jacqueline de Decker, may be contacted through the Missionaries of Charity
116 Burgstraat
9000 Ghent
Belgium
and the Link with the Contemplative Orders, Sister Nirmala M.C. may be contacted at:
1070 Union Avenue
Bronx
New York 10459
U.S.A.